THE

SEX

GODDESS

DIARIES

SERENA SKINNER

First published in 2019 by Onyx Publishing, an imprint of Notebook Publishing of Notebook Group Limited, 20–22 Wenlock Road, London, N1 7GU.

www.notebookpublishing.com

ISBN: 9781913206369

A CIP catalogue record for this book is available from the British Library.

Typeset by Onyx Publishing of Notebook Group Limited.

To all the beautiful women in my life who, throughout the years, have accepted me in all my moments of laughter and tears, through girls' nights, and the ever-lasting friendships that span the miles. You are my tribe and I love you all.

To my children who have endured the embarrassment of having a mother who puts it all out there.

And, most importantly, to my husband, who has put up with and tolerated every crazy idea I have had throughout the years, sat through and given advice during the girls' nights at our house on so many Saturdays, and who has chosen to love me through it all, even when it was hard. I love you.

CONTENTS

DISCLAIMER

This book is written as a tool to explore sexuality and sexual energy. At any given point during any of the topics mentioned, it is important to maintain safe, consensual sexual practice. This includes using condoms, gloves, dental dams, or any other item to protect yourself from STDs or unwanted pregnancy.

This book is not designed to give any medical advice. If you have any medical concerns, endure pelvic pain, have unusual vaginal discharge, or have any concerns about STDs or pregnancy-related issues, please seek the advice of your doctor.

INTRODUCTION

WELCOME TO THE SEX Goddess Diaries! I am so excited that you have chosen to take this journey of sexual evolution and self-discovery. This is an opportunity for incredible revelation and insight into the innate power that you, as a woman, hold every single day.

Now, you may be asking: who is this woman writing this? Who is she to tell me how to be a Sex Goddess? Well, I'm a wife, a mother, a daughter; I am your neighbor, your friend, your sister. I am a spiritual being. I am a lover.

I am a Sex Goddess.

Professionally, I am a relationship and sexuality coach who has been fortunate enough to reach thousands through my work. My Facebook page *Love by Design* has over 14,000 followers. I am also a nurse practitioner and medical provider that specializes in antiaging and sexuality through the American Academy of Anti-Aging for Medicine; I am board certified via The American Academy of Nurse Practitioners, and own a thriving private practice.

The Sex Goddess Diaries' purpose is to guide you through a process of sexual and personal self-discovery.

To become a Sex Goddess, it takes more than just knowing "sexy stuff": it takes knowing and understanding the power of being a divine woman who is comfortable in herself as an individual. We're going to get down to some nitty gritty concepts, and, to do this, it is essential that you understand that we are going to use a wide array of words—words like "pussy", "vagina", "vulva", "G-spot", "anal", "ass", "breasts", "tits", "penis", "dick"… You get the point. Whilst many of us are already comfortable with these types of words, for others, they may feel vulgar.

The goal is to move past whatever you feel about the word. Delve into the concept; explore; surrender. There is always an alternative for every word, and I encourage you to explore all the concepts in this book, using different words throughout this process. We must not limit ourselves just because of some words.

Who is it For?

You may be asking if this is really for you; maybe you haven't ever seen yourself as a Sex Goddess. I say that this is as good a time as any to discover who you really are!

The Sex Goddess Diaries is for any woman who is ready to explore her natural, inner sexual power. This is the deep-rooted healing energy that is inherently yours;

the power we were born with. We all have the capability to unlock this energy, and this book is the tool to help you open up to the possibilities and explore the power that is innate within you. It will bring confidence and power both in the bedroom and in daily life.

The only thing that I ask of you is that you are willing and open-minded: look at your sexuality though fresh eyes; awaken yourself to the possibilities; be ready to feel more than you are used to; push yourself further; love yourself harder.

When I say that this book is for any woman, I really mean it! It does not matter how old you are; if you are married or single; if you have children; whether you consider yourself to be physically attractive or not. This sexual energy is found within, and how we style our hair, the color or age of our skin, or how we dress, in the end, does not matter: what matters is our ability to embrace the power within each and every one of us. This internal sexual energy determines our flow; our release. The Goddess lives within.

And what about men?

Well, I certainly don't want you all to feel left out, as I think reading this book can certainly enhance a man's knowledge of a woman's sexual realm. I personally feel that a man who reads this book in its entirety will gain a full, detailed understanding of how any woman's sexuality works—right down to understanding how a woman's perception of herself, her views on sex, and any inhibitions she may have, can impact her sexuality. A man who understands these aspects of a woman, in addition to the intricate working of her physical sexuality, has the power to bring about the Sex Goddess within his woman—plus, any man who is open to exploring any of *his* aspects of sexuality that are discussed in this book has the potential to reach new levels of orgasmic pleasure—levels that may not have been understood before. Take the leap and delve into the Sex Goddess Diaries, and bring your sexual skills to a new level.

How to Use This Book

There is no secret recipe or designated speed to progress through this book: each of us has a completely independent journey to take, and we are all probably starting at different levels. There are some chapters that will seem like a breeze, whilst others will take extra work.

Be sure to start from the beginning and work through chapter-by-chapter. Oftentimes, the flow of the Sex Goddess journey builds upon the content of the previous chapter.

There are activities or challenges referenced throughout the book, with each providing invaluable insight into the process of becoming a Sex Goddess. These are designed to guide you through the process, helping you to set intentions and goals along the way. Plus, if you complete the challenges mentioned, you're going to have an amazing journey to look back over as a tangible way to see just how far you have come! In order to complete these challenges, please follow the link at the end of this book and download the workbook. This is your Sex Goddess Workbook, and I will instruct you when to complete a certain challenge by writing its corresponding page number. Simply turn to the written page number once you have downloaded and printed your workbook and complete the challenges as you go!

Don't feel rushed to finish a chapter—especially if it makes you uncomfortable; as a matter of fact, the more uncomfortable you are, the more time I suggest spending on that section. True growth occurs when we are most uncomfortable, being pushed out of our comfort zones and staring down the things we most often look away from. Everything that is done should be consensual, and should help you towards revitalizing and igniting your sexual energy. Look at these as an opportunity to become more.

An An opportunity to redefine yourself as a Sex Goddess.

SECTION 1:
SEX GODDESS 101

UNDERSTANDING THE REALM
OF THE SEX GODDESS

D EEP WITHIN A WOMAN, there is a sacred space which is often unseen and unfelt, waiting to be provoked so as to provide an escape from reality. It is a connection of mind, body, and soul, all for a ubiquitous divine experience that takes a woman beyond herself—even if only for a few moments. All-too-often, it remains hidden, just as some of the greatest treasures and mysteries of this world usually do.

This is the realm of the Sex Goddess.

On this journey, we must look deep within ourselves and be willing to peel away layers of our self-limiting beliefs, many of which having been ingrained in us from a young age.

To say that this is an easy task would be a lie; but as a Sex Goddess, you have to be willing to go against societal expectations of what women are expected to look, behave, and think like. You must tear away the misogynistic ideas that plague our culture and embrace the beauty and power of the true Sex Goddess.

We, as women, must support one another in this quest of sexuality and freedom to be who we are, without fear of name-calling and degradation. We must identify who our tribe is in this quest of life; those who lift us when we need it most.

A Sex Goddess can identify the difference between pleasure and ecstasy, as well as understand how to incorporate both into her life.

She understands that the very breath in our lungs hold power to control, excite, and soothe.

She understands the inner workings of her body, and how they attain sexual power and pleasure. She is not afraid of seeking more, sexually, from herself or her partner.

She knows that each orgasm is a doorway to ecstasy, and that there are many ways to get there, each with their own way of being unlocked.

When each of these are combined together, it is then that we begin to understand the realm of the Sex Goddess.

CHAPTER 1:
SELF-LOVE

The Goddess falls in love with Herself, drawing forth her own emanation, which takes on a life of its own. Love of self for self is the creative force of the universe. Desire is the primal energy, and that energy is erotic: the attraction of lover to beloved, of planet to star, the lust of electron for proton. Love is the glue that holds the world together.

—Starhawk

SELF-LOVE.

What comes to mind with those words?

No, I'm not talking masturbation here; I'm not even talking about pampering yourself (although we can all use some of that!). I'm talking about loving yourself, as you are, in this moment and every moment, completely and unreservedly. I'm talking about loving your body; your spirit; your mind. The whole package.

If you already do this, then go on ahead to the next chapter—but I'm going to take a stab in the dark here and say you are not quite there. This concept is where a lot of women lose themselves. Women, for the most part, don't know how to practice self-love; we are often too consumed with caring for others, tending to put ourselves last. However, before we are able to have a deep, intimate relationship with another person, we must first learn how to have one with our own bodies; we must become self-aware, loaded with love and acceptance, to such an extent that it would take an army to tear us down.

We live in a society where a mythical standard of how we view not only ourselves, but others in general, is set. We think we are supposed to dress a certain way; look a certain way; act a certain way. We try and morph ourselves into something that is uncomfortable when we don't fit into this societal box, social media, TV, movies, videos, and magazines all playing a part in our social conditioning to look or be a certain way.

Indeed, we have been bombarded with these sources and expectations since birth. We are told what is acceptable, pretty, proper, or desirable; we are told the qualities that would make a good wife, and, as little girls, we are regularly told to "be a good girl". Society grooms us from a very young age regarding our perceptions about women and sexuality in general, and yet it does not allow for the fact that humans are sexual beings, possessing sexual energy. This sexual energy is a life force found within all of us, and yet it is pushed deep down, hidden away like something to be ashamed of.

A woman stands out in blazing glory of feminine power and beauty is often rejected or characterized as a "bitch", "she-devil", or "maneater". They are judged, belittled, and criticized, oftentimes by other females. These women who practice regular self-love often and loudly are regularly called conceited, prissy, bitchy, and stuck-up; however, on occasion, we are also called confident, powerful, and classy.

The perception of the person who is *seeing* such expressions of self-love often dictates which kind of description these women get labeled with: if the one who is witnessing the self-love and admiration feels threatened, fearful, or jealous of what they see, they will lash out and give it a negative connotation. However, those who are comfortable within themselves already— often other women who have learned to practice self-love, no matter where they are in their journey—are the ones who shower other women with praise and encouragement for this type of behavior. Notably, there are, of course, men who praise these women as well, and it is these men who are certainly much more secure in who they are as a man; they are the ones who are not afraid of the power in women, instead embracing their Goddess nature, frolicking in the magic it.

As a Sex Goddess, we learn to look at ourselves for who we really are, in the bedroom and out in the world. We see and appreciate what is unique and beautiful about us as an individual, and we become confident in ourselves, without the need for validation from others.

We learn to see our age, and our wisdom that comes with our age, as an advantage, and not anything to look down upon. It is a full circle of Maiden/Mother/Crone; each phase of our life has its own unique beauty and purpose. The sooner women learn how to destigmatize self-love and to instead encourage and embrace the sexual being and power within each of us, the happier and healthier we will become.

Can you imagine an entire planet of women who are happy, confident, and sexually powerful? The female species would be unstoppable! And today, it begins with you: you have the power to bring about meaningful change. Radiance, love, desire... It's all achievable.

The big question, then, is how do you get there? Grab a pen or pencil; we're going to do a few activities. Be thoughtful and don't rush. I encourage you to complete this as a 30-day activity. After all, self-love doesn't come overnight for most of us; it's going to take a bit of persistence and dedication from you. It is also going to require self-reflection, and it will likely challenge your mindset. It will push you out of your comfort zone at some point. Be ready to face these challenges in this book head-on.

The goal of these activities is simple: with some exhaustive, crazy, unrelenting self-love, you will stop limiting yourself and the world, and claim the foundation of your Goddess powers. Rather than constantly focusing on what you *don't* like about yourself, or what you wish you could change, I want you to learn to embrace who you really are. Love yourself in its entirety. Embrace each and every aspect of yourself, from every little hair on your head, down to the nail on your pinky toe. The pursuit of acceptance begins in you.

SEX GODDESS ACTIVITY

Please turn to Page 4 of your Sex Goddess Workbook now and complete **Challenges 1-5**.

I encourage you to continue these activities beyond the 30 days; make them part of your daily routine in life. Write out new notes to yourself each week and post them around your house so you can see them. It's us and our self-love pitted against the societal conditioning that places us in a never-ending battle! Choose to fight for you, and, by doing so, you also fight for others. When you choose to love yourself completely and authentically, you will gain a deeper sense of self, gratitude, and happiness. And who doesn't want that?

CHAPTER 2:
SELF-EXPLORATION

*The Goddess doesn't enter us from outside; she emerges from
deep within. She is not held back by what happened in the
past. She is conceived in consciousness, born in love, and
nurtured by higher thinking. She is integrity and value,
created and sustained by the hard work of personal growth
and the discipline of a life lived actively in hope.*
—Marianne Williamson

SELF-EXPLORATION COMPRISES MANY
things; it is a wide approach that addresses not
only our bodies, but our minds, our experiences,
our perceptions, and our expectations. Our personal
reality should be tested and flexed upon. This is not an
exploration of what others think of us, but what *you*, as
an individual, see as being you; what *you* believe yourself
to be capable of. Everyone you meet will have a different
concept of the person you are, which is okay; you're
probably different around certain people. I'm sure you
are not the same with your mom as you are with a lover,
nor are you the same with a best gal pal versus your

boss. It is only with yourself that you do not portray a persona. You have a freedom to be you, and, sometimes, we don't look that closely at ourselves out of fear. We fear not being enough, or being disappointed. There is hesitation as we question if what we are will fit into that premade box of societal expectation. Well, guess what? It's time to throw that box out.

If we are able to continually imagine ourselves to be something, whether true at the moment or not, we are likely to start believing it. This phenomenon is called the Illusory Truth Effect: endless repetition leads to its being ingrained as truth in our minds. This concept is used very successfully in marketing and media. Another more metaphysical view of this is called manifesting, the concept of which being that your thoughts can create a physical reality: imagining whatever you desire and thinking about it as if it already happened, until it becomes a focused source of thoughts.

When we think about and believe in our visions and thoughts, we have the ability to deliberately create our own future. We can create who we are, and who we want to be. How do we do this, you ask? Energy. As with everything else on this planet and beyond, our thoughts are vibrations of energy. The Law of Attraction states that "like attracts like"; essentially, the energy that we put out into the universe will attract things of a similar energy. When we imagine ourselves or our lives as how we want them to be, and believe that these scenarios are possible, we emit that energy. This energy then, in turn, will attract back towards us, bringing in tow the life we seek.

It can be something as simple as imagining yourself as rich, or successful in your career. It can even be a strong belief that you are already a Sex Goddess, or that you are confident, powerful, orgasmic, happy, healthy, in a loving relationship. There is no limit to this concept.

However, in order to get there, we must first look at what we are and who we want to become.

Down to the depths of your most hidden parts is where I want you to go. Who are you when no one else is looking? Who do you wish you were? What do you want to achieve?

As we embark on this journey of self-exploration, we must look deep within ourselves and be truthful with our desires. Throw away the thoughts about what you think you *should* be, and focus on what you *want* to be, or what you already are, without fear, guilt, or shame. Embrace the essence of you.

By the end of this journey, I want you to exude radiant, joyful confidence, in who you are as an individual now and in the future. Women who have this are undeniably attractive, no matter what their physical features; people are drawn to them, mesmerized by the fact that they are what they *want* to be, and not what society tells them to be.

Knowing and accepting who you really are is liberating and powerful stuff, and if it's new to you, it can be kind of scary at the same time. You may not know all the answers right away, and that's okay; this is just the starting point. Life changes, and our views of ourselves change as well. What I thought of myself at twenty and where I just knew my life was going is a very different picture to what I now see now in my forties—but let me tell you, this version is *so* much better than what I ever imagined. The work of self-exploration is never ending: we must continually be observing what is new within us; know that change is inevitable, and learn to embrace it. Too often, women choose to blend in with the crowd, to avoid notice. This is understandable; it can be uncomfortable to put yourself under the inspection of your own eyes. But don't fret, my darling; soon enough, it will all be part of the natural flow of you.

Self-exploration adds a layer to the deliciousness of the self-love we started creating in the last chapter. I want you picture an amazing chocolate cake with multiple alternating layers of frosting and cake; it is deep and rich, yet so soft and luxurious. And this is what your self-exploration is creating: every time we add a layer of self-love, we need to dig a little deeper into self-exploration. Layer after layer, building this masterpiece with a little bit more self-love, and then some deeper exploration, before you finally become a delicious, scrumptious cake, oozing with goodness that everyone wants a piece of!

This may not be exactly what you were thinking when you said you were going to become a Sex Goddess, but discovering the depths of the Goddess is essential; it is foundational in understanding the realm of the future you, as a Sex Goddess. Without these transformational chapters, this would just be a book discussing techniques for sex; but by looking into who you are and learning to accept, love, and explore it, we are allowing your power to grow and nurture the sexual being that is hiding deep down inside.

Ordinary is everywhere. Make the choice to be an extraordinary Sex Goddess.

SEX GODDESS ACTIVITY

Please turn to Page 7 of your Sex Goddess Workbook now and complete **Challenges 1-4**.

CHAPTER 3:
FINDING YOUR TRIBE

If one person knows that she is not alone, she is empowered.

—Dr. Maya Angelou

FINDING YOUR TRIBE. THIS is such a fun part, in my opinion! By reading this book, you have automatically joined the Sex Goddess tribe (which, by the way, you can find and contact on Facebook!).

Our Facebook page is private, and provides a safe space for you to discuss anything with your fellow Sex Goddesses. Having a tribe like this provides clarity, opportunity, mentorship, and inspiration; we talk openly about sex, love, orgasms, masturbation, bodies, etc. It is for those who are excited about being a Sex Goddess, and who want to learn more from others.

Whilst it is awesome to be in our group, it is also important to have a tribe surrounding you in life—not just online. I want you to find other women who support and encourage you; your lifestyle and your choices. This group should also include women who have your back no matter what: the ones who will pick you up and dust you off when you have fallen flat on your face; the ones who will tell you exactly what you need to hear, at the moment you need to hear it, even if it is hard to listen to. Your tribe will be there for you at a moment's notice when the tears are falling and your heart is broken; they will be the ones cheering you on during the hardest challenges in life; and they will be the ones to celebrate when you succeed.

You may already have a few of these amazing women in your life, but I think we could always use a few more. I have had the amazing opportunity to have several women like this in my life, and, through the years, the moves, the miles of living cross-country, the marriages, the divorces, the raising of children, the new jobs, the progression through school, the diagnosis that changed everything, the night shifts, the deaths of loved ones, the ups and downs of life as we know it... These women have stood by my side. And I love each and every one of them for it.

Jennifer, Grace, Kelly, Tricia, Leigh, Melissa, Miranda, Francis, and Kristi are the women who would drop everything in a moment if I were to ever need them, and I would for them. This is a beautiful blend of women, each from a different thread of my life, all providing a woven blanket of love and support that gives a sense of security, warmth, and protection.

This is what I am wishing for you: to have your own beautiful, crazy, amazing tribe; to learn to weave your own blankets together, protecting and securing one another. As a woman, this is a greater gift than any material you can buy. It does not have to be a certain number of women, nor do they have to be a certain age, religion, or ethnicity, or have a specific kind of physical appearance. All that is needed is that each of them brings a fresh set of eyes; a different perspective into life. The number in my tribe grows as the years pass, as I hope it does for you.

Take the time to love and support your tribe as much as they love and support you. I guarantee I wouldn't have made it this far in life without my tribe.

SEX GODDESS ACTIVITY

Please turn to page 11 of your Sex Goddess Workbook now and complete **Challenges 1-2**.

Remember that your tribe is fluid; they don't all have to know each other. There have only been a few times when a larger group of these amazing women in my tribe have met up, during an event where several of them came from all over to support me.

I love them, thank them often, and contribute right back to their tribe.

P.S. Just search the name of this book on Facebook to find us.

CHAPTER 4:
DROPPING THE
MISOGYNISTIC BALL

We have been taught far more about shame than about our anatomy.

— Lynn Enright, Vagina: A Re-education

WOMEN ARE RAISED FROM a very young age to hide, look away from, or showcase disinterest in their bodies. Parents oftentimes believe they are doing what is best for their daughters to protect them, when in reality, the parents are most likely embarrassed to talk with their children and teach them about their bodies due to them raised in the same way. Here, we can see there is a vicious cycle present.

Parents' inabilities to properly teach their children about their bodies stem from multiple things, such as societal expectations, religious views, media, and so on. What they *don't* realize is that they are actually teaching their daughter(s) misogynistic views, then leaving them to fend for themselves as they try to figure out, on their own, what they should have been taught before they became a young woman. Women all have natural urges and desires, and yet they have not been taught to accept or understand them. These messages that we receive from a very young age become ingrained on a deep level, often becoming difficult to overcome in pursuit of accepting what is natural.

Women's body parts are often seen as sinful or shameful; we are told to cover up, especially when it comes to our sexual organs; that they are bad, dirty, or smelly. Then, as we grow into mature, young, attractive women, there is a flip to this ideology: our bodies are seen as an object, pornographic, or a prize to be attained. We expect that, in order to be loved or found attractive, we must meet certain criteria. This is a conflicting concept for a mind who has always been told to cover her body up, leading to thoughts like, "Am I a sex kitten, or am I supposed to be a prim and proper lady?"

These types of experiences can send slow, demeaning messages that can pile up over time, and there is great variation between women in terms of how they handle such messages. Indeed, on the one hand, we have had our mothers scold us for expressing any aspect of our sexualities and our places of worship tell us that temptation and lust is dirty, shameful, and a cardinal sin—and then on the other, there are the ideas that women who dress in a certain, "revealing" way are "asking for it", or that those who wear "too much" makeup are "whores", or that masturbation is "dirty". Women who are taught these misogynistic viewpoints as they are growing up, whether that be in childhood, adolescence, or young adulthood, take such teachings in without even recognizing the destructiveness of them, since they are so ingrained and made to be "normal" in society.

If you are still unsure of what I am talking about, take a look at the following list. Do any of these statements resonate with you?

- I have been told, or felt like, sex is dirty.
- I have consistent feelings of not being attractive enough.
- I feel like something may be wrong with me sexually.
- I feel guilty for having sexual desires or thoughts.
- I am grossed out or embarrassed by the thought of masturbation.
- I can't stop thinking about different things during sex.
- I fear what my partner is thinking about me during sex.
- I have difficulty relaxing mentally or physically during sex.

- I feel like it's my duty to please my partner during sex.
- I have bodily insecurities that keep me from having/enjoying sex.

If you have ever felt any of these statements, which I am 100% sure we all have at some point in our lives, you can bet that you have had the misogynistic ball dropped on you. This may have not been done with malicious intent, and was most likely done in an effort to protect you, but it has been done, nonetheless.

So, what do you do about it now? Well, now, you are in a position where you can work to break through these ideas that have been suffocating your sexual power. It is not always easy, and is oftentimes the hardest part of this process: you have to change your views about sex and learn to embrace the idea of your sexuality as a human; to find comfort in it. We must break through the barriers that have been placed upon us during our upbringing, because if we continue to view something as wrong, inappropriate, dirty, or shameful, then we are not in a position where we can truly enjoy it.

SEX GODDESS ACTIVITY

Please turn to Page 13 of your Sex Goddess Workbook now and complete **Challenges 1**.

CHAPTER 5:
SEXUAL ENERGY AND BEYOND

Once you have uncovered the secrets of mastering your sexual energy, you will feel a peace that you may have never known.

— Roberto Hogue

W E COME FROM SEX. Our sexual energy is foundational to our life force, energy, creativity, and passions. It is a sacred path within you, leading you down the path to personal power and expression.

If you were to ask any one of my tribe about my sexual energy, I am 100% sure that any one of them would tell you that mine is on-point. One of the things I hear them say to me most frequently over the years is that I "ooze sexuality". This is not something I actively *try* to do, nor is it an attention-seeking type of behavior. I am not talking about flirting, or wearing a low-cut shirt; it is just something that happens organically within me. The joy and comfort I have in my own skin and my own sexuality spills over into my daily life. It is my experience that women who have learned to embrace their sexual energy emit an electric vibe out into the world, and this is something that the people around them notice. They are probably not even doing anything related to sex; they may even be unaware of what they are putting out there. Regardless, that powerful energy causes people to take notice and pay attention. People naturally become drawn to them. Those who are comfortable in their sexual energy become very attractive, even if their physical appearance is not what society normally deems beautiful.

Even when I have hung out with women who are more beautiful by societal standards than I (thinner bodies; longer hair; bigger eyes... You get the point), people seemed to be more naturally attracted to me. This does not only apply in sexual relationships, either; people generally seem to want to talk to me and learn from me, and, in most cases, they seem to be relaxed and happy around me. It's the *energy* that they are drawn to; the moth to the flame, if you will.

This sexual energy is often described as "confidence" in women, and sometimes, it *is* confidence; women who have learned self-love and have engaged in that aforementioned deeper exploration of themselves are often the ones emitting their sexual energy at a louder frequency, oftentimes unintentionally. This, in turn, attracts more power and sexual energy back to them in accordance with the Law of Attraction; remember, whatever type of energy we put into the world is the same kind of energy that will be attracted back to us.

For those who have had a hard time finding a good, solid, loving relationship, the first thing I want you to do is to reflect on your relationship with yourself: your body and mind. Any negativity that we use to demean or belittle ourselves leads to us releasing a more negative sexual energy, which will, in turn, attract people who have a similar negative energy. This is something that can feel like an immense suffocating shadow.

Did you just picture an ex like I did?

Alternatively, if we use our energy to focus on loving who we are and what we look like, that energy will naturally attract positive, loving people. It may just happen that as you start on your journey to being a Sex Goddess, this energy becomes unleashed (which, by the way, is a good thing).

Sexual energy comes from deep within. It contributes towards our vitality, creativity, and sense of wellbeing. We all have it, ready and waiting to be recognized, but often, it has been pushed down; hidden; secured away to a comfortable place, where our growth and happiness can be hindered—not just in sex, but in everyday life. Women do this for several different reasons: maybe multiple people hitting on you throughout the week just becomes exhausting, and you don't want to deal with it anymore; maybe you grew up in a not-so-loving home, and hiding, in all forms, was the only way for you to feel safe; maybe you have endured sexual trauma, and you protect yourself by shutting it off or blocking it out; maybe you fear seeming promiscuous; maybe you fear rejection. Feeling unseen can be more soothing to those who have experiences like this; it's a safe place for them.

What you need to understand is that embracing your sexual energy is *good* for you. It doesn't mean you have to throw your coochie out into the world and dance around like a wild woman at a bonfire ritual (which honestly doesn't sound too bad to me, either); rather, it involves learning how to recognize the flow of this energy in a familiar way, using it to move beyond the perceptions that are out in the world. It's the ability to find the love that you deserve, feeling that energy flow through you and being able to draw it into you. It's kind of like one of those dimmer switches: we have the ability to turn it up or down. It can be muted to a minimal glow, or be shining oh-so-brightly.

Sexual energy relates to all the other aspects in our lives, too: when we are not blocking our sexual energy, we have a sense of happiness, vitality, love, and, yes, even confidence. However, when we choose to block this vital energy, we often feel secluded, alone, and drained; we don't know why people are not attracted to us, and the loneliness that ensues can become all-consuming.

We seem to be in a rut that we can't get out of. However, when used correctly, sexual energy can ignite a flame deep down within you, providing light and warmth within your soul. It is in you right at this moment, waiting for you to create a spark.

There are things you can do to help increase your sexual energy; it is often as a result of the things that we are doing, or not doing, in daily life, that we end up blocking our energy. Here are nine ways you can help to get your sexual energy flowing:

1. **Get Enough Sleep**. In much of society, sleep is undervalued; the whole "I'll sleep when I'm dead" concept has taken over and can cause a heap of distress. We choose to meet a deadline over sleep, in turn choosing our desire to achieve above our most basic need. We choose to go with less and less of what we need, losing out on what is considered to be one of the major ways that the body restores and heals itself. It is when our natural energies and hormones balance out that our bodies recharge and reset. Try getting a proper amount of sleep for about 30 days and see what happens.

2. **Meditate**. Mediation, for me, is a vital aspect of life. It has helped me even on my worst days, helping to restore a balance that can mimic some of the benefits of sleep. Additional benefits of

meditation include: reduced anxiety; reduced stress; enhanced self-awareness; a stabilized heartrate; stabilized blood pressure; and reduced pain. Who wouldn't want to experience any of these? And it doesn't even have to take up more than a few minutes of your day!

3. **Clear The Negative Energy You Can Control.** Every time I have worked with a woman, I have them clear away things they know to be toxic. It doesn't matter if this includes social media, a bad boyfriend, or a bad habit; cleansing what you can clears the negative energy, and will allow new and positive energy to flow in.

4. **Exercise Your Pelvic Floor.** Exercising and working your pelvic floor muscles stimulates your energy, from your root chakra upwards. The muscle contractions send signals to your brain, saying, "Hi! I am alive down here!" Of course, the exercise can also lead to more powerful orgasms, which gets energy flowing in itself.

5. **Socialize.** Humans, besides being sexual by nature, are also social by nature. When we are hanging out with people we like, our bodies release a cascade of hormones that help to reduce cortisol (our stress hormone) and increase oxytocin (our cuddle and love hormone). Both of

these hormone responses open us up to sexuality. Also, by socializing, we feel less isolated.

6. **Engage In Physical Activity.** Getting up and getting active stimulates all of the cells in our bodies, and also has the same effect as socializing when it comes to our hormones. Physical activity can make you feel more alive, can wake you up if you feel tired, and can energize you for several hours.

7. **Engage In Breathwork.** Breathwork is super important—not just for sexuality, but also for our physical and mental health. Good breathwork can control pain, slow your heart rate, and decrease anxiety, which is why it will always be incorporated into meditation. It is so very important, to the point where I have dedicated an entire chapter in this book to teaching you some different styles of breathwork.

8. **Masturbate.** The stimulation of your pussy in and of itself is an amazing way to increase sexual energy. If you don't want to have sex with a partner, masturbating is the way to go. Try visualizing energy flowing through your body as you do it, building a beautiful glow of sexual energy; then, when you orgasm, release the energy! Use the energy to make noise and body

movements as you orgasm. (In Chapter 14, we are going to delve into different ways to masturbate.)

9. **Have Sex.** What better way to move sexual energy than with sex? We have become far too easily distracted with social media or Netflix, or just feel we are too tired to really want to do it. But have you ever had sex even when you just felt like you didn't have the energy, and then all the sudden—*bam!*—you were so happy that you did? Of course, if you are already completing the other items on this list, your desire to have sex will be there more naturally.

SEX GODDESS ACTIVITY

Please turn to Page 14 of your Sex Goddess Workbook now and complete **Challenges 1-6**.

The purpose of these activities is to open your channels, to clear negative energy, and to get your sexual energy flowing. I promise you, if you do each of these activities for a week, you (and anyone near you!) are going to notice a *huge* difference in your sexual energy.

CHAPTER 6:
UNDERSTANDING PLEASURE
VERSUS ECSTASY

If your ultimate aim is just multiple orgasms, then I'm afraid you're thinking small. You're thinking way below your true sensual potential. Aim for ecstasy.

— Lebo Grand

PART OF THE SELF-DISCOVERY of your inner Sex Goddess is the learning of how to attain ecstasy.

And no, I'm not talking pleasure.

Pleasure can be identified as both a physical and neurological response, occurring when a touch or sensation is registered in the body and is perceived as feeling good. We can all have pleasure in even the simplest things: holding hands, kissing, receiving a massage. Even the smell of our favorite food gives us pleasure. Pleasure is very tangible, meaning we can usually pinpoint exactly what we are getting our pleasure from. The opposite of this would be pain or displeasure. Both pleasure and displeasure can come from the same kind of activity. Let me explain.

We have all experienced that amazing, sensual, romantic kiss that gives you butterflies and you think about for days. We have all also experienced the kiss that feels like they're going on a mining expedition down your throat in search of a lost city of gold.

Not quite the same.

Or how about when you have had your clit stimulated? Was it the oh-so-sweet tease of building, luscious pleasure with each passing minute, or did your partner immediately and repeatedly flick it, causing you to get aggravated? The pleasure or displeasure we received in such a situation was based on how the area's nerve receptors perceived the stimulation: too rough, or oh-so-sweet?

Ecstasy is something that is beyond; it is a sense of euphoria that transcends the body. It is often overwhelming and consuming in the moment. Ecstasy can transcend time and place; you move beyond its physical aspect. The current moment is all you are aware of, and you surrender to it—not in the way where somebody is going to dominate you, or in a way leading to your feeling of being oppressed, but the opposite: the surrendering of yourself, for yourself. Of letting go of control. Your body trembles in anticipation. You are ready, releasing that which may hold you back. You move beyond expectations to experience something greater. Breathe it in; become lost in it. Ecstasy. A multileveled experience, where you may feel like you are floating, weightless. It can be found during an orgasm, if you allow it, and in the afterglow that follows an orgasm.

Ecstasy is the experiencing of a sensation in our bodies and in our spirits. Ecstasy entails a feeling of something beyond our physical body, extending into a realm outside of our ordinary experience. Pleasure is in the body; ecstasy allows the energy of the universe and all of its potential to transcend to you, even just for a moment.

We can have pleasure without ecstasy, but it is difficult have ecstasy without pleasure.

When I speak of ecstasy in the context of the Sex Goddess, I am not talking about the feelings we get from drugs, or alcohol, or adrenaline; these simulate a faux sense of ecstasy—an easily bought and readily available faux ecstasy, at that. These false sensations confuse the moment (that is, our innate capacity to facilitate a journey through ourselves to a deeper level of our beings).

So, how do we work on being able to attain ecstasy?

1. **Be In The Moment.** Move out of your mind. Don't think about going out to dinner, or about your to-do list. Be completely in the moment of

now. Feel everything. You must be ready and willing to do this at several times during the process; we often become too aware of other matters, and our minds will move us out of the moment. We must learn to recognize this and choose to remain present, over and over again.

2. **Let Go Of Expectations.** Once you learn to give up expectations, you open yourself to so much more. Transcending ecstasy takes you deeper and further. If you are setting expectations, you are not allowing yourself to experience the moment as it is; if you are looking for it to feel or be a certain way, you may be blocking the ability to go further. If we are setting up expectations of what our ecstasy is supposed to be, we are very likely to miss when it has the potential to actually entail.

3. **Move Beyond Control**. Surrender. I touched on this briefly above. Oftentimes, surrender is a scary thing; it takes us to a potential unknown. It requires vulnerability; for you to accept whatever is happening, and to just allow it to happen. We can't force an orgasm, or be worried about how we look, or what sound we make, in that moment. Don't be a part of the moment; *belong* to the moment. *Be* the moment.

4. **Breathe**. Controlling how you breathe helps to keep you in the present, allowing you to go deeper. Breathing is an automatic response in us from the moment we are born; it can make you feel dynamic, and is viable to your energy flow. As I have already stated, breathwork is a huge component in this book; it plays such a vital role in everything we are working to attain.

5. **Be Willing To Receive.** The full depths of a sexual experience can take you to a new level of ecstasy with new opportunities for letting go. To reach this level, you need to accept your lover's gifts; you must be open and able to willingly receive what your partner is trying to give you. The ability to receive this moment requires you to completely let go—of wandering thoughts, the past, control, and, of course, expectations.

Generally speaking, women tend to face difficulty in applying just one of these concepts, much less putting them all together at the same moment to be able to attain a high level of ecstasy. But *imagine if you could.* Imagine *when* you can. I'm sure you can at least envision it: you are lying back, enjoying your partner. There is nothing distracting you. This moment is the only thing that exists. You graciously accept the physical pleasure you are experiencing. Everything feels unbelievably amazing, and you give in to yourself, releasing all expectations, fears, and thoughts. You take a deep breath and revel in the moment, sipping in the sensations before you like a delicious, full-bodied wine, dizzying and intoxicating; full of ecstasy.

Sounds tantalizing, doesn't it?

If you are anything like most women, then learning how to throw yourself into complete release may be a challenge. You may have to work on one concept at a time, or you can try several of them at once. It is whatever feels right to you. Go ahead; give in to ecstasy.

SEX GODDESS ACTIVITY

Please turn to Page 20 of your Sex Goddess Workbook now and complete **Challenges 1-3**.

CHAPTER 7:
BREATHWORK

*Breathing in, I calm body and mind. Breathing out, I smile.
Dwelling in the present moment, I know this is the only
moment.*

— Thich Nhat Hanh

*Breathe deeply, until sweet air extinguishes the burn of fear in
your lungs and every breath is a beautiful refusal to become
anything less than infinite.*

— D. Antoinette Foy

I KNOW YOU ARE probably thinking that breathwork doesn't sound very Sex Goddess-like, but believe me, it is. Our breath oftentimes controls the flow of our internal energy. It is essential to life and movement, to the point that our bodies instinctively do it without us even thinking about it.

Often, our breath matches our emotions, feelings, and physical exertion; it matches pain, pleasure, fear, and contentedness. We can even alter our own emotional or physical feelings by recognizing what our breath is doing and altering the flow toward something that more closely resembles what we desire.

Think about it: when you are upset and have been crying, your breath, without thinking about it, becomes shallower and more uneven. This increased respiration then sends a physiological response to your sympathetic nervous system, or our fight-or-flight response. Our heartrate will increase, muscles will tense, and, often, a flood of hormones will rush over us, prompting the whole cycle to continue.

On the other hand, think about what happens when you take slow, controlled, deep breaths when you are upset. It may take a minute, but your body responds: slowly, you start to come off the edge of the emotional rollercoaster and, before you know it, you are able to think more clearly. Your heartrate is down and your muscles start to release their built-up tension. Controlling our breaths allows us to control many physical and emotional aspects of ourselves, switching us over from our sympathetic to our parasympathetic nervous system. And guess what? Our parasympathetic nervous system helps to control our sexual arousal.

Who are my Yogis out there? If you have ever done yoga, you have experienced how important breathwork can be. It is integrated into every practice; in fact, breathwork has always been seen as a connecting source between the physical and spirit, and it is the most tangible representation of vital energy, known as "prana". Prana is believed to be the lifeforce that animates the entire universe. Defined in this way, breathwork should be viewed in terms of having utmost importance during sex... Don't you agree?

We're going to learn four different conscious breathing techniques. Conscious breathing is exactly what it sounds like: we are actively thinking about and controlling our breaths, as compared to our natural subconscious breathing that takes place without thought, even when we sleep.

If need be, practice these breathing techniques alone, if you are a little self-conscious about it. Soon enough, you will recognize the benefits of conscious breathwork, and will become more comfortable practicing at different times and places. However, to begin with, sit or lie in a comfortable position. Try to have few distractions around you when you begin practicing all breathwork. It is also a good idea to set a timer so you don't have to worry about keeping track of time.

Breath of Bliss

This is a very basic, deep-connecting kind of breathing that helps to regulate your body towards the parasympathetic pathway. It is done to slow and connect

our conscious mind to our body, as well as to bring
awareness to how our breath feels and moves through us
in the most basic way. Practice for 3-5 minutes.

1. Sit or lie in a comfortable position
2. Close your eyes and place one hand on your
   tummy; the other hand can be anywhere that is
   comfortable. (I like to put mine over my heart.)
3. Start to become conscious of your breath: the
   movement of it; the feel of it in your lungs.
4. Keeping your eyes closed, take a slow, deep
   breath, in through the nose. You should feel your
   tummy rise with your breath and then your chest
   as you inhale completely
5. Hold for a few seconds.
6. Slowly exhale through your mouth, allowing the
   breath to make a releasing *ahh* sound as it leaves
   your body.
7. Notice that your tummy went down with the
   breath.
8. Slowly start to take another breath and start the
   cycle over again.

I'm guessing that you are feeling pretty relaxed now!
This technique can be used at any point during the day
to help you to slow down and relax a little. It is a good
idea to practice Breath of Bliss before any sexual
activity, as it will help to prime your parasympathetic
nervous system, to calm any racing thoughts, to reduce

stress, to relieve muscle tension, and to allow you to focus on the sensations of your body. All good things when it comes to making sex more enjoyable!

Circular Breath

Circular Breath is having a continuous movement to your breath, without interruption: no pause to hold a breath like you did with the Breath of Bliss. It is a continuous flow, in and out, your breath flowing in a synchrony of inhale, then exhale. It is not a difficult technique to use, but can be very powerful in circulating erotic energy. Practice this for 5 minutes.

1. Sit or lie in a comfortable position.
2. Close your eyes and place your hands wherever they are comfortable. (I tend to place mine in the same position as the Breath of Bliss.)
3. Relax your mouth and throat, allowing them to open. Your lips may be parted.
4. Slowly become aware of your natural breath.
5. Begin taking a deeper breath through your open mouth, feeling the air pass through your throat and into your lungs as your diaphragm expands.
6. Allow your breath to be as deep as feels comfortable. Do not force it.
7. Without pausing, begin to release your breath, keeping your mouth relaxed and slightly open.

You should take the same amount of time to exhale as you did to inhale.

8. Once your exhale is complete, do not pause; immediately begin the cycle again.

As you are doing this, I want you to imagine a golden light: as you inhale, it floods down to your lungs and diaphragm, all the way down your spine and down to your root chakra. Then, as you exhale, let it work it ways back, trailing along through your pelvis and navel and back into your lungs... And exhale it out. Imagine a beautiful golden circle of energy orbiting through your body as you breathe in and out. It is normal to feel a warming sensation, or even a surge of emotion, whilst practicing Circular Breaths.

This is a great breath practice to do alone, but it can also be incorporated before or during sex with your partner. It is a good way to synchronize your sexual energy. The flow of breathing is exactly the same as if you were practicing by yourself. There should be a continuous circular flow of breath from both of you.

Either before sex or during, consciously gaze into each other's eyes. Find a matching pace of breathing; then, as he breathes out, you breathe in, taking in his energy. Then, when you exhale, he inhales, keeping the same pace and flow of energy. After your breaths are in-sync, imagine the golden energy from your partner being absorbed into your lungs: with you; with your breath. Focus and draw that energy all the way down to your root chakra as you inhale. As you exhale, your golden energy flows out, back into your partner's body. As your partner breathes in, he should imagine taking in your sexual energy, moving into his root chakra before drawing it back up through his body and breathing it back into you to complete the circle.

This is a powerful sexual tool to incorporate that will increase the degree of pleasure and intimacy experienced for both of you.

Breath of Fire

The Breath of Fire technique originated in Kundalini Yoga. It is a highly energizing breath that has been shown to cleanse the lungs and sinuses, energize the body and mind, and help the body to heal and build strength—and, as you will see, to magnify a sexual response. Breath of Fire uses your diaphragm to pump new breath rapidly in and out of your lungs in a steady rhythm that is very similar to a dog panting. Notably, this is *not* the breathwork to practice if you are looking to relax and calm down; it is made to energize and focus. It has been shown to reduce toxins in the lungs, increase endurance (definitely a win with a Sex Goddess!), reduce pain, decrease food cravings, and more. Pretty impressive, huh?

Contraindications

Breath of Fire can be risky for certain individuals. If you have cardiac problems or high blood pressure, any spinal disorders, have a respiratory infection, or vertigo, you should not practice Breath of Fire. If you're pregnant, don't not practice Breath of Fire. Start this practice for 30 seconds and work your way up to 3 minutes. Here is how to do Breath of Fire:

1. Sit up tall, with a straight spine. Place your hands on your knees with your open palms facing up towards the sky and your eyes closed.
2. Slowly, start noticing your belly expand with each inhale and contract with each exhale.
3. Pinpoint your navel in your mind. Breath of Fire is focused from the navel point (or the solar plexus), and the diaphragm is used to pump the navel in and out with each inhale and exhale.
4. Start with doing one full breath every two seconds.
5. Once you find the rhythm in the movements of your breathing, open your mouth and begin to pant like a dog, increasing the amount of breath flowing through you. Keep a steady pattern.
6. Now close your mouth and continue breathing through your nostrils at the same pace.

7. You may quicken the pace of the inhale and exhale, but keep them equal. There is no pause between the inhale and exhale.

8. Try to breathe at a rate of approximately 2-3 cycles per second.

When done correctly, your chest will remain relaxed and slightly lifted, and your hands, feet, face, and abdomen will also be relaxed.

Please Note: If you feel dizzy or lightheaded, you can slow the rate of your breathing. Also, pay attention and ensure that both the inhale and exhale are of equal duration. Keep your practice short in duration to begin with and work your way to longer times.

Breath of Fire moves and unblocks a lot of energy within your body, and can have physical symptoms. There are many different sensations that you may experience, but it has been noted as common to experience the following:

- A tingling sensation on your face, neck, hands, or feet;
- A feeling of lightness at the top of your head;
- A warming sensation in your second chakra, just below the navel down in the sacral chakra, in the pelvis area;
- Flashes of color during, even if your eyes are closed.

Don't worry; as I already said, these are common to experience, and resolve themselves pretty quickly once you are finished.

Congratulations on learning one of the most transformative breathing techniques! I'm sure you are seeing how big a part this breathwork plays into our sexuality. By learning to harness powerful breath—that is, focusing in our second and third chakras—we learn to harness sexual energy.

Orgasmic Breath

This one is definitely one of my favorites! This technique immerses you into your own experience. It can help you to feel more sensual and to build orgasmic energy. Saying this, you can't be worried about how you look or sound, or what your partner is thinking when you practice this technique; rather, you must allow yourself to drop all concerns and immerse into your body, remaining aware of your sensations and what you are feeling.

There is a flow to it that combines parts of all three (Breath of Bliss, Circular Breath, and the Breath of Fire): there is an awareness and control over the breath as it flows in the same as the Circular Breath; and your breaths are done in a faster tempo, similar to the Breath of Fire. It does not have to be as fast as the latter, but it is definitely faster than Circular Breath. I encourage you to incorporate body movements and sounds: push your breasts out, or even stroke them as you take a deep inhale. Let's break it down.

1. Sit or lie in a comfortable position. Your eyes may be opened or closed.
2. Begin the same as Breath of Bliss: start to become conscious of your breath, the movement of it, and the feel of it in your lungs.
3. Take a slow, deep breath in through the nose.
4. Hold for a few seconds.
5. Slowly exhale through your mouth, allowing the breath to make a releasing *ahh* sound as it leaves your body.
6. After a few cycles, transition to Circular Breaths. Relax your mouth and throat, allowing them to open. Allow your lips to part.
7. Become aware of your natural breath.
8. Begin to gradually increase the tempo of breathing, having a continuous flow in and out. Ideally, you may reach 1-2 breaths per second.
9. As you reach a steady tempo, inhale while pushing your breasts out, or even stroke them as you breathe deeply into your root chakra.
10. As you exhale with each breath, make whatever sensual noise that wants to come out of you naturally whilst releasing your breasts back down.

You are almost making and undulating movement with each inhale and exhale.

11.Start to become fully aware of the sensations going throughout your body, accepting them and the sounds you are making. Do this for as long as you desire, and then slowly start to ebb the flow and energy.

With the practice of Orgasmic Breath, there is a chance you will reach orgasm. Even if you don't have an actual orgasm, often, women feel the "afterglow" that many experience from an orgasm. It is a wonderful technique to incorporate into masturbation, and, of course, into sex with a partner.

Breath, sound, and movement open you up to more sexual energy, vibrancy, and bliss. Take the time to work on each of the techniques in this chapter. If none of these make you feel anything, I encourage you to get a book or take a course on breathwork. Find one that works well for you. For these listed here, I would suggest working on the first three individually, learning control and technique until it becomes second nature, thereby making the Orgasmic Breath a sensually mind-blowing experience when you combine them all together.

SEX GODDESS ACTIVITY

Please turn to Page 23 of your Sex Goddess Workbook now and complete **Challenges 1-3**.

SECTION 2:
ANATOMY

CHAPTER 8:
ANATOMY

*As for your backrubs... Study an anatomy book, pal, because
what you've been rubbing isn't my back.*

— Susan Elizabeth Phillips, What I Did for Love

I KNOW WHAT YOU'RE thinking: "She can't really be about to tell me that I have a vagina." I think we can all agree that we all know and understand the general concept of what your anatomy—pussy, vagina, whatever you want to call it—is like; however, what *I* have come across in my years is that many women really don't take the time to get super-familiar with their selves in a very personal way. It's like you are great at being acquaintances with yourself, but do you really have a heartfelt, loving relationship?

When you picture someone or something you love, you can see them in your head, right? You can sense the shape of their face; their hair color; perhaps the way they sound or smell. Imagining this person can bring a smile to your face. So, tell me, can you do that with your own pussy? Can you do it with your lover's pussy or penis?

Can you visualize the intricate shape of it, both when aroused and not? Have you ever stopped to really appreciate your own intricate femininity?

I find so many women are often afraid to look at their own bodies. A friend of mine was over at my house one night, having a few drinks. Of course, we were having a conversation about sex. It was a conversation about how much more comfortable I was with my body and sexuality than she was. She was a single, beautiful woman of about 35 at the time, and it was this night that I realized that a woman the same age as me, with the same capabilities for sexuality, had never in her life even looked at her own pussy!

And she had three kids!

To say I was surprised was an understatement; I guess I had always just assumed that women were curious and looked at their own bodies. Needless to say, I immediately found a hand mirror and sent her marching into the bathroom to go and have a look.

At 35 years old, for the first time, my friend sat and really looked at her pussy. I sat in the kitchen waiting for her return, wondering what she was thinking; how had she gone this many years being a sexual creature, without ever looking at it? Did she knew she had a beautiful, glorious, and powerful pussy that had never been celebrated? She wouldn't have known that the appearance of it changes when aroused, swelling and almost blossoming like a flower offering its nectar to the source of its excitement. It explained a lot of why she felt she was missing out on some of her own sexuality. I also found out that, because she did not have a loving relationship with her own pussy, it was difficult for her to let someone *else* have that relationship. Let me tell you, it was game on! I started working with her to understand and explore her sexuality, and today, she is a Sex Goddess! It was not an overnight process, but it was absolutely amazing to watch the journey unfold.

I can also guarantee you that, after working as a healthcare provider for many years, people really don't know squat about how their bodies really work! I have been amazed at some of the things that people have told me: one person firmly believed that women pee out of their vagina, and another did not think she had a cervix, because she didn't know what it was. One woman told me she wasn't pregnant because she didn't want to be. Yes, after spending this many years in healthcare, I have seen and heard it all!

We are going to take a detailed look at the female structures for sexual pleasure, such as the vulva, the clit, and the vagina. I am not focusing on reproductive anatomy such as the uterus, ovaries, and fallopian tubes, nor will I cover the anatomy of the breasts, since this is the body part women are much more familiar with, as we interact with them daily. I will keep this section as brief and as interesting as possible, although it is important to bear in mind that I never just assume that everyone understands their body anymore! We are also going to go over some of the male anatomy, so when it comes time to shower them with some pleasure, you will know exactly where to go to take them to heaven! Ready?

CHAPTER 9:
THE VULVA

I bet you're worried. I was worried. I was worried about vaginas. I was worried about what we think about vaginas, and even more worried that we don't think about them.

— Eve Ensler, The Vagina Monologues

THE EXTERNAL FEMALE GENITALIA consists of the vulva, which is all-encompassing of the different parts. Most often, we hear it talked about as a "pussy" or "vagina". Pussy is an all-encompassing term as well (one that I have come to find endearing), whilst the vagina is technically a specific structure. The vulva includes the mons pubis, clitoral hood, clitoris, urethral opening, labia majora, labia minora, the vaginal opening, the perineum, and the anus. Check out the image below and identify each part.

Anatomy of Vulva

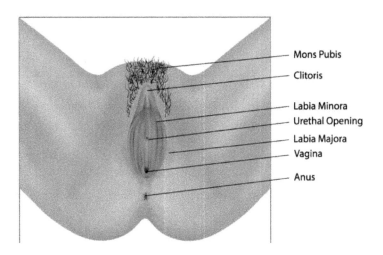

One of the beautiful things about the vulva is that whilst we all have them—all with the same structures and functions—they are each beautiful and different in their own way. Our pussies are as individual as we are in every other way when it comes to the size of the labia, clit, and vagina, as well as the color, hair distribution, texture, and so on.

A magnificent expression of how beautifully different our vulvas are showed up in 2011 when UK artist, Jamie McCartney, revealed his five-year vulva-sculpting project. Here, he had 400 different women volunteers pose to have a mold of their vulvas taken.

The resulting plaster casts were then assembled into a wall sculpture, showcasing the exquisite, delicious differences that women possess. His work is a 30-foot sculpture that is broken into 10 panels, titled *The Great Wall of Vagina*—and it has been a hit all over the world! Have a look at his work.

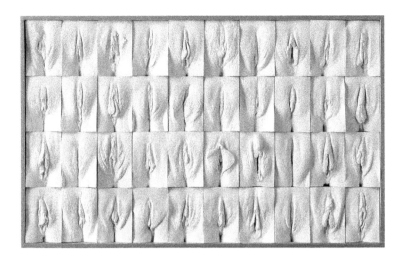

(Photos Courtesy of JamieMcCartney.com)

You see that none of them look the same? There are differences in the shapes of the labia and clits, and they will change even more with sexual arousal. What's crazy to me is that there seems to be a cultural standard for what a pussy is supposed to look like: smooth in color and texture, with minimal hair and a "neat, tucked-in" appearance. But this standard of pussy only accounts for a very small portion of the beauty that is out there, and denies the absolute differences we all have. Which brings me back to my point: do you know what yours looks like?

You need to have a detailed understanding of your pussy to be able to harness its full potential. Know what it looks like at different times, such as during arousal; how your skin tone changes color; the size of your clit; the fullness or flow of the lips. By seeing your vulva as a masterpiece and understanding that it looks different from everyone else's whilst at the same time looking similar, you gain power, appreciation, and, hopefully, a fascination for your pussy.

SEX GODDESS ACTIVITY

Please turn to Page 27 of your Sex Goddess Workbook now and complete **Challenge 1**.

CHAPTER 10:
THE CLITORIS

The clitoris is pure in purpose. It is the only organ in the body designed purely for pleasure.

— Eve Ensler, The Vagina Monologues

THE MYSTICAL AND MAGICAL clitoris; the primary source of female orgasmic pleasure; the part of the female genitals that eludes much of the male species, as far as understanding its depths and possibilities goes; and, as stated in the quote above, the only organ in the human body that is designed to give pleasure, and nothing else. It is also known as:

- Clit;
- Bean;
- Butter Bean;
- Boy in the Boat;
- Button;
- Clitoris;
- Devil's Doorbell;
- Happy Button;
- Jewel;

- Kernel;
- Knob;
- Little Man in the Boat;
- Lovebud;
- Love Button;
- Nub;
- Panic Button;
- Pearl
- Skittle;
- Sugar Plum;
- Sweet Spot.

In my opinion, it is the most adoringly named body part that we have. Whatever you call it, we can all agree that it is important... Well, *all* our parts are important, but this one especially loves attention. It's that ever-elusive nub that you can find when you spread your outer lips, or the labia majora. Unless you are aroused, you will most likely need to pull the clitoral hood back to get a full view of your clit. Even still, what you are able to actually see is just the tip of the orgasmic iceberg.

The clit is actually a fairly complex bundle of nerves, blood flow, and tissue—and, like our male counterpart, it, too, can become erect with arousal. Now, I'm not saying that you're going to get a full-on erection that you can see from across the room, but it *does*, in fact, swell and become larger, protruding out and becoming more sensitive. Let's take a look so we can get a better understanding.

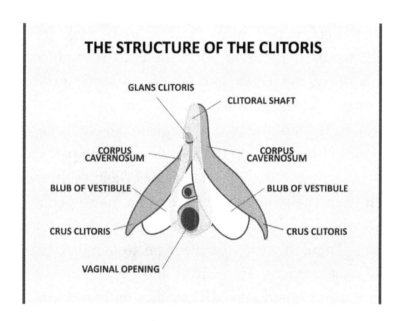

THE STRUCTURE OF THE CLITORIS

This is the all-encompassing clitoris as we understand it today. The only part we are actually able to see when we look at the female anatomy is the glans clitoris, which is covered by a protective layer of skin called the clitoral hood.

It wasn't until around 1998 that the extent of the clitoris was more widely understood. Prior to that, the glans clitoris was, as a general rule, the only portion illustrated in anatomy textbooks. It was often described as a malformation of male genitals.

Yes, really. Not exactly an appealing description!

It wasn't until Australia's first female urologist, Dr. Helen O'Connell, who disagreed with what she had read in textbooks whilst in medical school, took it upon herself to really discover what the clitoris entailed. She first explored the female genitalia by dissecting cadavers for direct visualization, and it was at this point that an understanding of the diagram above first came into being. She was able to identify all of the parts as we know them today and label their functions, which are actually similar to those of a man's penis. This is also why I said earlier that it can become erect with arousal. Then, in 2005, she went on to demonstrate and prove the exact structure and function of the clitoris, using functional MRI studies on live women.

Can I just stop for a moment and say, let's give this woman a round of applause! I had already had my second child before the medical community had a full and complete understanding of the clitoris; I hope you're as appalled by this as I am! It's not like I was born in the 1800s, after all. The clit deserves better than that!

Standby for a bit of a nerd anatomy moment.

The internal part of the clitoris is connected to the glans by the clitoral shaft, which extends into the corpora canvernosa—two spongey areas of erectile tissue. A little way down the corpora cavernosa, it branches into a pair of wings known as the crura. The crura extends into the body and around the vaginal canal, sort of resembling a wishbone, and can be as long as 9cm on each side. This is an important aspect, as it kind of gives a hug to the vagina, but also plays a part in the other female mystery: the G-spot. But more on that later.

Underneath the crura are the clitoral vestibules, or vestibular bulbs. Like much of the clitoris, these sac-like structures of tissue become engorged with blood when you get aroused. The clitoris structure as a whole is estimated to have—wait for it—over 8,000 nerve endings.

Wow.

I bet you had no idea your clit was the badass, powerhouse, orgasmic organ that it is! And not only that, but it is estimated that those amazing 8,000 nerve endings, just in your clit, interact with about 15,000 additional nerve endings in the entire pelvis. It is the Sex Goddess metaphorical iceberg, if you will, with 90% of its mass laying beneath the surface, concealed.

Clits come in various different sizes, and, whilst in the same general area, it is found in a slightly different place from woman to woman: some are much more hidden than others, and it can also grow or change with age or hormonal changes, such as pregnancy or menopause. Plus, as already stated, when aroused, the clit becomes engorged, becoming larger and easier to identify.

Now, let's go back for a moment and talk about the G-spot. There is an abundance of controversy out there about this other elusive source of pleasure, but, as we just discovered, the G-spot is actually an internal area of the clitoris that wraps around the vaginal canal. The distribution of how it wraps around and hugs the vaginal canal, in combination with the varying distribution of nerves between woman to woman, is a key factor as to why there is no one identifiable position for G-spot stimulation: the variability of our nerve endings and the sensation that an individual feels is often not the same from day-to-day, or even moment-to-moment. However, this is not to say that it is impossible to find; we are going to learn a little more on how to stimulate the G-spot a little later. For the purpose of this chapter, I just wanted you to have an understanding of the anatomy of it.

By the way, I am not expecting you to remember all of the parts and functions of the clitoris; I just want you to appreciate and understand the beautiful complexity of what you've got down there. Indeed, the purpose here is to become *familiar* with your clit, intimately. It is then, and only then, in the disruption of the quiet as you discover the magnitude and ability of your clit, that you start to become one with your inner Sex Goddess.

Welcome to the Cliteratti.

SEX GODDESS ACTIVITY

Please turn to Page 28 of your Sex Goddess Workbook now and complete **Challenges 1-4**.

CHAPTER 11:
THE VAGINA AND THE CERVIX

Why do people say 'grow some balls'? Balls are weak and sensitive. If you wanna be tough, grow a vagina. Those things can take a pounding.

— Betty White

I AM SURE IT is apparent to you by this point that when I say vagina, I am talking about a specific part of your female anatomy. Here are some of the other names that are well-known and, in my opinion, quite humorous:

- Vag;
- Vajayjay;
- Box;
- Nether Regions;
- Lady Business;
- Lady V;
- Hoo-Haw;
- Cha-Cha;
- Lady Bits;

- Crotch;
- Muff;
- Kitty;
- Cooch;
- Cooter;
- Snatch;
- Snapper;
- Beaver;
- Cookie;
- Cupcake;
- Coin Purse;
- Lady Flower;
- Honey Pot;
- Poon;
- Punani;
- Twat.

The list can go on and on.

Take a look at the photo below. This is a full picture of the female reproductive system. Why? Because the vagina by itself in a photo doesn't always make a lot of sense.

Female Reproductive System

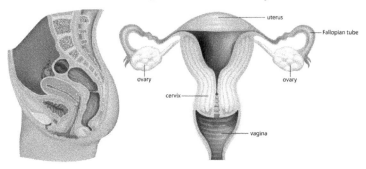

The vagina itself starts at the vaginal opening, located in the vulva, and extends up to the cervix, or the ending of your uterus, as seen in the picture above. When not aroused, the vagina is approximately 3.5 inches in depth and 1-2 inches wide.

The walls of the vagina, which are pleated and called "rugae", are designed to elongate, stretch, and widen to accommodate objects, meaning it can take a penis, fingers, toys, and even a baby, when called to action. When not actively engaged in accommodating an object, the vagina is what we call a "potential space"; essentially, it collapses down onto itself—so, if you have ever thought of your vagina as being an open space inside of you go about you day-to-day life, think again. Here's the best visual I can give: it's like that shirt we threw on the floor, all piled up on itself, folding in however it landed. It is not standing up in "perfect shirt" form.

When aroused, the vaginal walls swell by approximately two inches, and the upper portion of the vagina elongates, pushing the cervix and uterus deeper into your body to make room for penetration. Once it has done this, the vaginal canal is approximately 6-7 inches, doubling its depth in anticipation of penetration.

Now, as mentioned previously, there are about 15,000 nerves that make up the pelvic region. The first two inches of the vaginal opening contain the largest amount of these nerves in the vagina, accounting for the pleasure we experience from "just the tip" and during initial penetration.

Now, let's have a conversation about vaginal secretion (or lubrication): the vagina is a mean, lean, self-cleaning machine, being highly functioning in flushing out cells, excess fluids, and bacteria. It works to self-regulate its pH based on where you are in your cycle, maintaining an average pH of about 4—which, by the way, is equivalent to a fine wine—whilst at the same time providing a hostile environment for semen. During ovulation, your luteinizing hormone surges, causing your vagina and its secretions to have a pH of about 7 or higher. This is to allow for a for a happier environment for sperm to survive for the purpose of conception. After ovulation is done, your hormones shift again, and the pH once again comes down to about 4. Hence, normal vaginal secretion changes depending on where you are in your cycle; even if you have had a partial hysterectomy (where they take out the uterus but leave the ovaries), your body will still have hormonal cycles that control vaginal secretion.

These secretions will go from not-very-lubricated to super-slippery, the latter occurring during ovulation so as to allow for a more hospitable environment for the sperm to reach the egg; it then turns to a creamy white, and then to a kind of chalky, drier feeling right before menstruation. All of these are a normal part of the vagina's daily operation, and have nothing to do with getting wet during arousal.

The lubrication that we get when aroused is caused by small, pea-sized glands located near the lower vaginal opening, called Bartholin's glands; so, if you are laying face-up on a bed, these glands are located on either side of the vaginal opening, closest to your back (near the perineum).

You also other glands in the front vaginal wall, usually between the G-spot and the distal end of the urethra, near the vaginal opening. These are called the Skene's glands, and, when lying face-up (in the same position that we discussed for the Bartholin's glands), the Skene's glands can be found at the vaginal opening, closer to the tummy. These glands have been found to play a key function in female ejaculation/squirting. We're going to go into female ejaculation later, but for now, I just need you to know the anatomy.

The anterior vaginal wall, or the inside of your vagina that is located on the tummy side, is often where many women can locate their G-spot—typically about 2-3 inches inside the vaginal canal. Due to the angle of where it is most commonly found, the majority of women either require a toy for self-exploration, or a partner to help (preferably one who can follow directions!). Deeper inside of the front vaginal wall is the anterior fornix, also known as the A-spot. This is another area known for pleasure when stimulated, and is located a few inches above the G-spot, between the cervix and the bladder.

Another quick point to mention (as I have had the question asked a hundred times before): the vagina is not open to your abdominal cavity. So, whilst you can't technically "lose" anything in there, items can be pushed deep enough that you may have difficulty retrieving them. But not to worry: a quick trip to the gynecologist and that tampon can be out in a jiffy. Notably, if at any point you are concerned about your vaginal secretion (such as if it changes color to gray/green/yellow), or if you have pelvic pain, be sure to get checked out by a medical provider.

As stated above, the cervix is located at the end of the vaginal canal, and is located at the bottom of your uterus. It is a small, donut-shaped structure that is firm to the touch. You may have already felt it if your partner has hit it with a penis or a toy during intercourse. It is highly vasculature in nature, and, whilst not weak structurally, it can become bruised from intercourse and repeated hitting of it. For many, the cervix may be tender due to a condition called an "armored cervix", which may cause pain or discomfort when stimulated. This condition can be the result from several different situations, including physical trauma (e.g., pap smears; rough sex; childbirth; emotional trauma).

The cervix acts as the door/passageway between the vagina and the uterus; however, it has also been shown to play a role in some orgasms. You can see where the cervix is located in the image provided. It is also possible to locate your cervix manually: to do so, you will need to sit in a comfortable position (like on the end of a bed, a toilet, or in a squatting position). It is going to be easiest to locate it when you are not ovulating or midcycle, or right before or after sex, as the position of the cervix will change based on hormones and sexual arousal. Once you have gotten into position, insert your index or middle finger deep into your vagina in somewhat of an upwards motion, and feel for a slightly firm object amongst the soft give of the vagina. Your cervix can be deeper inside than you initially think; hence, if you don't feel it, don't despair. It may take several tries before you actually figure out where your cervix is. If you feel something firm that doesn't have much give, you have probably found it. If at any point this causes you discomfort, or you feel you may have an armored cervix, stop what you are doing and breathe. Later on in this book, we will discuss the ways to work beyond an armored cervix—but at this point, for the purpose of anatomy, all I want you to do is understand where it should be.

There can be some anatomical differences in where a cervix is located: whilst most come more at a downward angle, some of them can be "tilted", or at an upward angle. Some women have even reported having *two* cervixes. If you have had a hysterectomy, there's also a pretty high chance they also took your cervix during the procedure, and the whole finding-your-cervix experiment is not gonna be your thing.

SEX GODDESS ACTIVITY

Please turn to Page 29 of your Sex Goddess Workbook now and complete **Challenges 1-2**.

CHAPTER 12:
THE MALE ANATOMY

I don't agree with Freud's theory about women having penis envy. Don't get me wrong, gentlemen; your penises are great. I'm just not personally interested in possessing one myself. To be honest, the last thing I need is to worry about the size of another one of my body parts.
—Jenny Baranick, Kiss My Asterisk - A Feisty Guide to Punctuation and Grammar

THE MALE ANATOMY. IT is the most adored body part by all who possess it; a prize gifted to them in the form of an XY chromosome. In keeping with the spirit of the anatomy chapters, let's have a look at some of the other names:

- Dick;
- Cock;
- Manhood;
- Schlong;
- Dong;

- Heat-Seeking Moisture Missile;
- Sexcalibur;
- Member;
- Meat;
- Johnson;
- Fuckstick;
- Wiener;
- Shaft;
- Willy;
- Beaver Basher;
- Cum Gun;
- Danger Noodle;
- Boner;
- Tool
- Pocket Rocket;
- One-Eyed Snake;
- Prick;
- Funstick;
- Krull the Warrior King;
- Sausage;
- Joystick;
- Pecker;
- Rod;
- Custard Launcher;

- Disco Stick;
- Knob;
- Wang.

The list goes on, and on, and on—with 386 slang terms, to be exact, the majority of which focusing on the penis itself. But enough of that: the purpose of this chapter is to explain the concepts of the male anatomy needed by a Sex Goddess.

You will find that many men will often resist some of the ideas that we put forward in the pleasure section of this book, whilst embracing others that are more "socially acceptable"; either way, the information will be yours for your disposal. It will be up to you to find a man who is adventurous enough for a Sex Goddess. Men who can put aside their preconceived notions may find absolute enjoyment in the types of orgasms they can experience by the exploration of *all* their male anatomy. So, on with the lesson.

For our education, we are going to focus solely on the parts dedicated to sexual pleasure, including the penis, scrotum, perineum, and prostate gland.

Yes, you read that right.

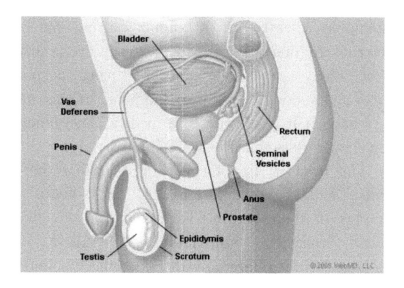

Penis

The penile shaft is composed of three column-like chambers of erectile tissue, similar in nature to that found in the clitoris. These make up the length of the shaft. The urethra goes down the middle of the penile shaft. Each of the two larger chambers on either side of the penis is called a corpus cavernosum, and, together, these make up the bulk of the penis. The corpus spongiosum, which can be felt as a raised ridge on the erect penis, is a smaller chamber that surrounds the spongy, or penile, urethra.

Side note: A man can fracture his penis during intercourse. This is usually during a rapid and missed attempted re-entry into a vagina, causing the corpus cavernosum (one or both of them) to rupture. A man will most likely experience extreme pain, a popping noise, and sudden bruising to the penis. If this were to ever happen, it is considered a medical emergency, and you should go to the closest ER immediately.

The head (or tip) of the penis is called the glans penis, and has approximately 3,000-4,000 nerve endings (or about half of what is found in the clit). The direct repeated stimulation of these nerve endings during intercourse increases the likelihood of ejaculation.

The frenulum is located on the underside of the head of the penis, where the glans joins the shaft. This is considered to be a very sensitive part of the penis for the majority of men.

Penises can be one of two ways: circumcised, or uncircumcised. In the latter group, there is a layer of skin from the mid-shaft that extends down over the head and forms a collar, called the foreskin. This also contains a dense concentration of nerve endings. Meanwhile, circumcised men have had the foreskin surgically removed. Cultural and religious beliefs are the two main reasons for circumcision. Neither is right or wrong.

Scrotum/Testes

The scrotum and testes, more commonly known as the "balls", is another well-accepted portion of the male sexual organs. The scrotum, or the "sac", is a highly pigmented, muscular sack that extends from the body behind the penis and hold the testes. The testes, or the "nuts", are typically about 4-5 cm in length and produce both sperm and hormones (e.g., testosterone), and are active throughout the reproductive lifespan of the male. They make him capable of impregnating a woman at any age after puberty.

Perineum

The perineum is the skin between the anus and scrotum in the male (and between the anus and the vulva in the female). This will part will become more important in a just a minute.

Prostate Gland

The prostate gland is an internal gland about the size of a walnut, and is formed of both muscular and glandular tissues. It excretes a milky fluid that collects the sperm coming from the testes, the combination of sperm and fluid from the prostate gland then becoming semen, or, as most of us know it, "cum". To directly feel the prostate gland, you must access it through the rectum.

For men who have had a vasectomy, this is basically a disruption in the pipeline between the testes and the prostate gland and, thus, when these men cum, it only contains the fluid from the prostate gland and no actual sperm.

The Male G-Spot

The male G-spot is basically a combination of the prostate gland and the perineum. For men, the perineum is especially sensitive due to there being a small patch of nerve endings beneath that are in direct communication with the prostate gland. When stimulated correctly (either directly on the gland or indirectly, through the perineum), men are able to have a different kind of orgasm called a prostate orgasm. We will cover this topic in detail in the orgasm section.

Bonus Material (just because knowledge is badass to have!):

Cowper's Glands

A portion of semen is made by two glands called Cowper's glands; these release a thick, salty fluid. Sound familiar? This fluid lubricates and prepares the urethra for ejaculation, or "cumming". The fluid from these glands is released after the male becomes sexually aroused and before the release of the semen. It is most commonly known as pre-ejaculate or "pre-cum".

It is important to note that it is possible for this pre-cum to pick up sperm already present in the urethra, and thus may be able to cause pregnancy. This is why the "pull out" method is unreliable.

SEX GODDESS ACTIVITY

Please turn to Page 31 of your Sex Goddess Workbook now and complete **Challenges 1-2.**

SECTION 3:
PLEASURE

CHAPTER 13:
SELF-PLEASURE

*It's more than a bath; it's a transformative experience.
You're searching for buoyancy in the soul, and spring in
your step.*

—Amy Leigh Mercree, The Mood Book: Crystals,
Oils, and Rituals to Elevate Your Spirit

I N THIS CHAPTER WE are going to discuss different ways to explore self-pleasure. Notably, masturbation, as what we all think of as the main form of self-pleasure, has its own dedicated chapter following this one; here, however, we are going to talk about other ways to perform self-pleasure—kind of like foreplay, only with yourself. This is limited only by what you think, and it can be different for everyone: ritualistic, exotic, or soothing. What I think surprises people the most is that this doesn't even have to be overly sexual: it can be anything that makes you feel sensual, happy, beautiful, comforted, and/or spiritual; it is anything that allows your body to be more attuned for when sex happens. If we are too pent-up, anxious, worried, distracted, or anything other than relaxed and open, our sexual energy becomes hindered.

If you remember from Chapter 6, pleasure can come from numerous things, and is what leads us to ecstasy. So often, we, as women, are so busy taking care of others that we neglect ourselves. You know that saying, "You can't pour from an empty cup"? When was the last time you spent a day doing pleasurable things for yourself, without attending to someone or something else? No multitasking; no phone calls or text messages; no work; no children; no to-do list; nothing? What about even *half* a day? Such a time doesn't necessitate no one at all being with you; it just means that you are not expected to do anything for them.

Imagine your best day: you have been able to sleep in, and, when you awaken naturally, you can get some coffee or tea, shower, and get dressed before heading out. You grab a muffin or something on the way to the spa, or even meet your tribe for brunch prior to going. You arrive at the spa and are greeted, being offered a sparkling water or mimosa as you sign in. You are then whisked away to the back for a pleasurable day that could include a facial, full-body massage, and waxing. Maybe your day also consists of a hair and makeup appointment, or even with just sitting by the pool. After the spa, you find yourself roaming some cute little boutique shops and find an amazing outfit that looks stunning on you. In the evening, you have a dinner date planned, and you put on your new outfit before heading out. You and your date go to a chic restaurant that you have been wanting to try: the atmosphere is beautiful, and the food is a whole new experience for your mouth. Maybe you decide to go dancing afterwards and have a few drinks, and, when you get home for the evening, you are happy and fulfilled.

I am guessing that, after a wonderful day such as that, you are much more attuned with your sexual energy; the relaxation and happiness that has filled you throughout the day has led to a replenishing of your cup. I am aware of the fact that the day I just described also requires money, but you can make your day into whatever you wish it to be; this was just an example. You could do a day that doesn't cost anything extra, and, again, it can be anything that feels good to you. I used to live in a house that had a very secluded backyard with a high fence, and, during the summer, I would lay out on a large beach towel, topless, or sometimes completely nude. I loved the feel of the sun on all my skin, especially the areas that didn't get to see sunlight very often. I would have some music playing, a cooler with some cold drinks within reach, and even a kiddie pool to lounge in when I got hot. I loved the change of temperature and sensation from hot sun to cool water on

THE SEX GODDESS DIARIES

my bare breasts; I felt completely free and sensual in those moments where I reveled in the feel of my own skin. I was happy, with no requirements of me, except to be in the moment. After spending the day in the sun, I would go in and take a shower—you know the ones that feel so amazing after a day at the beach, or pool—and dress in some light, comfortable clothing. My husband and I would either cook at home or go out to eat, and then spend the evening together.

Self-pleasure is whatever feels best to you: it can be spending the day nude, taking a hot bath, massaging your own breasts, getting a new haircut, reading a book, masturbating, cooking, going to the beach, shopping, getting a massage, going to a salt therapy room, yoga, meditation, dancing in the kitchen, watching a movie, or going on a bike ride or a hike. It is anything where you feel good in your mind, body, and soul once you have finished. It is my opinion that every woman should have a minimum of one full day a month dedicated to this type of self-pleasure—and, if you are a man reading this (which, by the way, I think *all* men should), I implore you to make this happen for your Goddess. The return will be tenfold, especially if she feels like she doesn't have to ask or fight for it. Make it happen for her; she is worth it!

Relax the mind; revive the body; renew the soul.

SEX GODDESS ACTIVITY

Please turn to Page 34 of your Sex Goddess Workbook now and complete **Challenges 1-2**.

CHAPTER 14: MASTURBATION

Masturbation is a mediation on self-love. I would recommend and intense love affair with yourself.

—Betty Dodson

Among all types of sexual activity, masturbation is, however, the one in which the female most frequently reaches orgasm."

—Alfred Charles Kinsey,
Sexual Behavior in the Human Female

MASTURBATION: ONE OF THE more policed activities and morally shunned experiences of female sexuality. It is one where women are frequently scorned, and it is never spoken of, even amongst other women, for fear of judgment or being seen as some kind of sexual delinquent. It has always amazed me how accepting society has been of male masturbation, yet for females, the concept is often entirely rejected—unless, of course, it is the topic of a woman scorned; that is, one who has developed a hatred for men and has replaced the male species entirely with vibrators; or, alternatively, in pornography, where the entire concept is displayed solely for the pleasure of those who gaze upon it, rather than for the woman's own pleasure and discovery.

Female masturbation has always had its obstacles: during the 19th and early 20th century, women who learned how to orgasm through the experience of masturbation were classified as having a "psychological deviance", and automatically deemed as a medical problem—and yet during the 19th century, female hysteria was often treated by doctors with a "pelvic massage" (also known as genital stimulation) so as to achieve "hysterical paroxysm" (or what's known by you and I as an orgasm).

Pretty contradictory, don't you think? It's no wonder women are often conflicted with the concept.

As young women, we are often uncomfortable with the ideas of masturbation and pleasure within our own bodies; yet how are we expected to know and explain to our partner what we like, if we do not know how to attain it ourselves? With this in mind, let me tell you something about being a Sex Goddess: you are going to find new, beautiful ways to have sex and pleasure yourself. That's right; I want you to masturbate!

We are going to start by exploring the different ways of masturbating. If you have never masturbated before, this is going to be a chapter where you are going to make *huge* gains as a Sex Goddess—that is, if you participate accordingly! Before we do, though, let me state up-front that there is no wrong way to masturbate: as long as it feels good to you, you are doing something right. Saying this, I want you to be open to all different kinds of masturbation, and to explore every kind.

This chapter is dedicated specifically to hands-on masturbation. We will cover toys in the next chapter, which you can always incorporate into your masturbation sessions; but for now, I want you to become familiar with the feel of your own breasts, nipples, and magnificent pussy. I want you to notice the softness of your skin; I want you to touch yourself completely and freely. Every woman is a little different, and what feels best to you may not feel the same for someone else. Don't be afraid to alter the techniques, either; everything we are going to cover is general guidance. Be open; be wild; make *noise.* I want you to find your orgasm!

For years, there was no consistent verbiage for the different techniques that could be used in female masturbation. It took OMGyes.com to come along before this ceased to be the case, being a website entirely dedicated to exploring female pleasure through research. They have interviewed thousands of women aged 18-95 concerning how they reach sexual pleasure, and what they have consistently found is that many of the women all had similar techniques, and yet no set way to describe or talk about it. This is where they began to build a language that is used on their website today, teaching pleasure in a common language. In their first season, they go over 12 techniques that are used to enhance pleasure and reach orgasm. Their content includes instructional videos, as well as interviews with different women on what they learned during their self-pleasure discoveries. There is absolutely no way that I can cover all the content they offer on their website here, and so I highly encourage you to get a membership to their site. It's a onetime cost for each season, and well worth the price, if you ask me.

Instead, here, we are going to cover a few of the techniques that I have found to be incredible. Remember that this chapter is all about hand stimulation—no toys. Feel and explore yourself on a whole new level.

Rhythm
The rhythm technique uses sensation in a repeated pattern, and it's this concept of rhythm that makes vibrators so popular. Repeated rhythms can be done with rubbing or tapping with fingers across the clit using different pulsation rhythms. As sensation and pleasure start to increase, our pace and rhythm may increase as well. When masturbating, we often use a

combination of rhythms and build as we go. Let's go over some of the variations to see what I mean.

Skipping

This variation has a simple and steady approach in consistently skipping a beat in the pattern. It is great as a starting rhythm in your masturbation session, and allows time for increasing pleasure. It also allows time for you to take notice of the different sensations. There is no rush here: if you maintain this pace, it can build a delicious frustration that achieves an oh-so-sweet release of orgasm in the end.

Raindrops

This technique calls for a variation in the pattern. It can be stimulating and exciting to mix up the flow of clitoral stimulation, and tells the clit that it can't adjust or adapt to the sensation. This can heighten pleasure for many women, although it can be frustrating for many. Figure out what feels best for you.

Back-To-Back

With this variation, the fingers have a fluid, continuous movement, with no pause between motions. This pattern ensures a steady, continuous sensation, without losing any of the building pleasure.

Constant Pulsating

This pattern is often done near and during climax. It is more of a continuous humming or fluttering sensation: your fingers never leave the clit with this rhythm. It is not meant to be slow, but is still very deliberate. In this rhythm, orgasm is the goal, and is not necessarily included in the journey to it. This is often the technique women use during sex with a partner to ensure they reach orgasm. Practicing this technique may be helpful when it comes to sexual intercourse later on with your partner.

Edging

Edging is one of my favorite techniques, and works to increase pleasure by approaching orgasm and then easing away before it happens. You use self-stimulation, getting close to orgasm before retreating and holding back, only long enough to start the process over again. Repeatedly nearing orgasm, but stop before it happens. This builds longer, more intense orgasms for 65.5% of women. There are also three variations of edging that works well for most women.

Variation 1: Pausing, Going to Zero, and Rebuilding
In this style of edging, you stimulate yourself near to orgasm and stop completely, bringing your orgasm back down to zero. You can do this in a few minutes, or you may choose to wait a few hours; whatever works best for you. The key in this variation is to wait until the urge to orgasm is completely gone, and then starting over, building near to orgasm again before stopping, as you did before. You can do this as many times as you choose, and each time, the intensity behind the orgasm will increase. This technique can often take more time, but ultimately can lead to some of the most intense orgasms.

Variation 2: Distracting the Orgasm Away

In this variation, as you near orgasm, make a sudden change in placement or sensation away from the clit to distract and fade away from orgasm. After a few moments of distraction, the impending orgasm will have faded, and you can then work your way back to increasing pleasure. Again, you can do this as many times as you like, building and increasing intensity as you go. Some women feel an increasing pleasure throughout their entire pussy as they build during this technique, their entire pussy pulsating with pleasure before orgasm.

Variation 3: Continuous Edging

In this style of edging, play with your clit, building yourself as close to orgasm as you can without pushing yourself over the edge; then, shift your touch away from the clit. Feel or touch something else on your body that still provides intense pleasure, but is not directly on the clit. You may try stroking up and down the vaginal opening during this time. After the intensity of the impending orgasm fades down (but not completely away), return to the clit and star the cycle over again. Continuous edging is an ebb and flow of pleasure, fluid in sensation and flow, keeping you more engaged during the entire process.

As with any of the techniques that we discuss in this chapter, there may be some challenges; some of the more common ones with edging include passing the point of no return unexpectedly and not being able to stop and withhold the orgasm. Meanwhile, other women tend to lose orgasms, being unable to easily build them back. In this case, the technique can become frustrating, but just know that there are several techniques to try; you will find the one that works best for you in no time.

P.S. Edging is my personal favorite; it builds to a *spectacular* orgasm.

Orbiting

This one is described by OMGyes.com through the idea that there are "a million ways to circle the clit". Now *that's* the way to get some attention! This technique is simple, yet complex in itself. Let explain what I mean.

When we are practicing orbiting, we make circular motions around, and on, the clit, applying varying degrees of pressure. There is a huge variety in the "styles" of circle that can be applied here, as well as in what feels good during one moment; indeed, a previously enjoyable sensation may become aggravating in the next moment based on the individual and their ensuing sexual response—not to mention the difference in women's preferences, too. There is an extensive nerve bundle beneath the clit (as we learned in the Anatomy section) that extends deep into our genitals; thus, when we practice orbiting, different sections of the nerves get stimulated, as compared to just stimulating the clit itself. Generally speaking, there are four areas for orbiting. Let's go over them.

The first (and least intense) style of orbiting it to encircle the clit without ever directly touching it; you can glide your fingers above and to the sides of the clit, kind of like making half-circle patterns around it. The clitoral hood remains in place, covering the clit, and the motions go around your nub without ever directly touching the clit. This is a good pattern for overly sensitive clits, the nearby stimulation of the nerves sufficing for orgasm.

The next level of orbiting follows a similar pattern, but can include actually going over the clit whilst it is still covered by the hood, increasing the stimulation without directly touching an exposed clit.

As we progress through orbiting, we can continue the patterns of circling, using half-circles or figure-eights, occasionally exposing the clit from under the hood and gliding across it in the process. However, it is important to note that just because the clit may be exposed now does not mean we should bombard it:

THE SEX GODDESS DIARIES

continue a circular flow to and away from it, providing small breaks of direct stimulation.

The last level of orbiting is called "Direct Hit", and is for when the clit is ready for a more aggressive approach to stimulation. This is where the clit is fully exposed, with the hood pulled back, and you repeatedly encircle it. This is definitely not a first step to take when it comes to clitoral stimulation.

The amount of pressure applied to each of these variations of orbiting is also going to be down to personal preference; I want you to take the time to explore the different orbiting techniques with different pressures. Try mixing them up a little and find a variation that pleases you.

Orbiting is one of the techniques that you will gain a much deeper understanding of by joining OMGyes.com; their exceptional videos and infographics on this amazing website will take your understanding to the next level!

Shallowing
This is the last concept we are going to touch base on in this amazing chapter on masturbation.

Shallowing explores masturbation beyond the clit: here, we explore the sensations and joy of touching just inside the vaginal opening. There are a ton of nerve endings in this opening; after all, how many of you have been with someone and, as they were just about to penetrate you, they held off, giving you just a taste of the tip? Did you like it? Did it build anticipation? Well, that's the concept here.

The first few centimeters into the vagina have an incredible sensory pattern, and, compared to the rest of the vagina, has a very delicate sensation. There's a whole different level of pleasure in this area, if we can learn not to rush past it. How we learn to use it in masturbation can help us to lead our partners during sex; indeed, OMGyes.com reports that 82% of women can achieve extra pleasure by stimulating the vaginal opening. It's as though this simple act of shallowing awakens and stimulates the rest of the vagina for what's to come (pun intended!).

Shallowing can be done in a few simple ways: it can certainly be done with a penis or a vibrator, but I still want you to start with your fingers; I want you to be able to explore your own pussy, and how it feels beneath your touch. Saying this, many women notably do prefer this technique with a toy or partner, since it can provide a more complete sensation to the vaginal opening.

To mix this up a little: the "fluttering" technique of shallowing provides a gentle knocking at the door. Here, you can take two or three of your fingers and just gently push at the vaginal opening repeatedly, without inserting.

The "tipping" variation, meanwhile, follows the same pattern of fluttering, but with a slight insertion of the fingers—just the tips, if you will. This sensation primes your body for "more", and, quite frankly, feels amazing! I love, love, love to combine shallowing with different styles of clitoral masturbation for a completely erotic, mind-blowing experience!

I hope even reading through this chapter has turned you on with the idea of being able to touch yourself in different ways to experience different kinds of pleasure. It may also take several tries (darn!) to get better at each technique, but I encourage you—no, I *implore* you—to get that membership to OMGyes.com; they have so much more to offer in terms of tips and advice on learning women's pleasure. Once you learn which techniques work the best for you, teach them to your lovers.

Remember, being a Sex Goddess in your own right includes understanding and knowing how your body experiences erotic, unrelenting pleasure; it's not just about what kind of pleasure you give to someone else! It is essential to experience different kinds of stimulation so we can learn what our bodies like. By doing this, you will be in a position where you are able to tap into the sacred sexuality flowing in you, as well as to voice what you want to your partner. Masturbation allows you to connect to the lifeforce within, helps you claim and understand your sexuality, can allow you to heal prior misogynistic concepts, and allows you to harness the power that is in every woman.

SEX GODDESS ACTIVITY

Please turn to Page 36 of your Sex Goddess Workbook now and complete **Challenges 1-2**.

CHAPTER 15:
TOYS & MORE

Even if times are tough and you're enduring a terrible heartache, it's important to focus your anger on a vibrator, not another person.

—Chelsea Handler

I N THIS CHAPTER, WE are going to go over several of the different kinds of toys—specifically, those that can be used in sexual pleasure. There are all kinds of toys for different purposes, and they come in all kinds of shapes, sizes, colors, materials. There is no shortage in manufactures, either. All toys can be used in masturbation or with a partner during sex. The taboo of owning a sex toy is not what it used to be: long gone are the days of shame for even thinking about having one, much less talking about it; yet oddly enough, there is still a large amount of people who really don't know where to begin. Let's start by talking about four points to consider when finding a great toy of any kind.

1. **Make sure it is made of safe materials.** Any sex toy that you decide upon should clearly state what it is made of. Some of the earliest sex toys were made of porous materials that would harbor bacteria, or be laden with different chemicals. However, over the course of the last decade, the sex toy industry has upped its game in line with the growth of consumer knowledge. Silicone, glass, and stainless steel are three of the most popular materials currently, all of which being non-porous, able to be sanitized, and not harboring hidden, unsafe chemicals (e.g., phthalates). If you are not sure what your toy is made of, ask—or move onto one that is clearly marked.

2. **Ensure there is an understanding of anatomy.** Companies who make sex toys should have a functional understanding of anatomy; after all, a "one size fits all" approach will not work when we are talking about what people want or need. Just because something *could* go in a vagina does not mean it will *function well* when it comes to pleasure. There should be some understanding of how the toy would work on a real body, as well as an array of available sizes to choose from. It should also be ergonomically correct for the purpose; a standard dildo is not as functional

when trying to stimulate a G-spot, for instance. This is not to say this can't be done; it is just done more efficiently with a proper toy, designed with that specific purpose in mind.

3. **Ensure there is plenty of feedback.** Read the reviews! Look for companies that have great reviews from independent sources (meaning not on their own website). The majority of people who post reviews do so in an honest nature in the hopes of making someone else's shopping experience better, and, in the era of online shopping, looking for reviews on anything has become standard procedure. If you're going to spend the money to find something to make your pussy (or any other body part) feel magical, make sure it's worth buying!

4. **Look for innovation.** There is more to a quality toy than just how big it is! Look for innovation, or some indication that there was a sensible thought process behind the design that addresses common concerns. This could mean it having an ergonomically shaped handle, quality craftmanship, buttons that are well- designed and placed. It should overall be easy to use, and not break within the first few months of use. No one wants to get frustrated with the functionality of a

THE SEX GODDESS DIARIES

toy! This is another aspect you will find to be covered when you read those reviews.

I am going to go over some different kinds of toys; I can't assume that everyone is familiar with each of these! What we are going to explore below are some of the most popular categories of toys out there on the market. For a look at some of my favorites, just check out my website SerenaSkinner.com, or check out the reference section at the end of this book. I recommend masturbating with and without them, as well to stay in-tune with your body and the ways in which you/plan to direct your partner in giving you pleasure.

Dildos

Dildos are devices that are shaped similarly to an erect penis, and are used in a sexual way to promote pleasure. This is most often through the penetration of the vagina and the anus. People who enjoy the feeling of being penetrated, or enjoy the feeling of fullness in their vagina or anus, are most likely to enjoy this type of toy.

They can be of any length or amount of girth, from ones that are two inches all the way round, to ones that are monster-sized, requiring two hands to fully wrap around it. Further, whilst dildos are designed to simulate a reduced version of the sensation that comes from real penis penetration, that doesn't mean that all dildos look like realistic penises: they come in all shapes, including animals, rockets, wands, twists... Pretty much anything you can think of.

They can also be made from a variety of materials, with some of the most common ones including PVC, silicone, stainless steel, crystals, and glass. Rubber dildos are not as popular, since the jelly rubber that was most frequently used contained phthalates, which have been found to be linked to several health problems. If you do have a rubber dildo, it is recommended by health providers that you use a condom with it. Silicone is currently a very commonly used material, and is resistant to accidental damage, non-porous, and easily sterilized, making them more durable and sanitary than dildos made of softer materials. Glass dildos are solid, with no give, and can be a solid block of color or multicolored. They are most commonly made of Pyrex or other types of borosilicate glass. Glass dildos can be warmed or cooled to provide a varying sensation.

Vibrators
Vibrators come in a variety of options: they click, thrust, shake, twirl, suck... You name it! They are an endless buffet of sexual stimulation. Standard vibrators are very similar to dildos in shape and size, and are most often silicone-based so as to allow for the vibrating

THE SEX GODDESS DIARIES

mechanism to remain inside the toy. They can be used for vaginal and anal stimulation, although there is a whole genre of anal play toys out there, which we will get to in just a bit.

The standard vibrator is usually phallic in shape, and is designed for penetration. Many have different features, such as a clit stimulator, or, as it is often called, a "rabbit vibrator". These vibrators have an external section that usually resembles rabbit ears (hence the name) that provides vibration to the clitoris, whilst a second section goes inside the pussy for internal stimulation. This type of toy works well for those who still like penetration, but need or want additional clit stimulation. There are also dual anal and vaginal vibrators, which follow the same concept of dual stimulation.

There are clit stimulator toys that fall under the vibrator category, which are usually designed directly for clitoral stimulation (no penetration). With the use of air or sonic waves, the clit receives a kind of stimulation that can be absolutely mind-blowing. Many women have found a new level of orgasm with these small but powerful options: they often describe the sensation as being similar to being eaten out, but better. Those who find enjoyment from traditional vibrators also tend to be quite fond of this category.

Bullet vibrators obtained this name due to their cylindrical shape, and are considered by many a gateway sex toy. They are often bought as a first toy, since their small size make them appear less intimidating. Initially designed for clit stimulation, they are actually pretty versatile, and can be used to stimulate multiple different body parts, from the nipples to the nether regions. Bullet vibrators are great for travel due to their size and how easy they are to conceal.

Not all bullet vibrators are shaped like bullets, and can take on a sly form. I think my favorites are the ones made to look like lipstick, making it so you can carry this little bad boy anywhere. Another plus is that there are a lot of dildos or cock rings that are designed with slots to fit a standard-sized bullet, in case you want to up your pre-existing sex toy game. Another fun aspect to them is the fact that they can come with remote controls, making them super-fun for couples.

G-Spot Wands

G-spot wands can fall under the dildo or vibrator category, one of their key features being their shape: the majority of G-spot wands require more of a curvature, as well as a more distinct level of rigidity, in order to be effective. They have an expertly positioned curve that allows them to reach the all-too-often unattainable sweet spot on the front of your vaginal wall, or the G-spot. Without the proper curve, it becomes more of a challenge to hold your toy at the correct angle. I have yet to meet a woman who can reach her G-spot with a hands-only approach to masturbation. Hence, the more rigid nature of this toy will hence allow you to apply more pressure to your G-spot for maximum stimulation. Whether you have one that vibrates or not is completely down to your personal preference.

One really popular G-spot wand—and my personal favorite—is the Pure Wand from the company NJOY. It is a stainless-steel, heavy-duty bad boy that easily reaches the goal. This one does not vibrate, but that has never been a problem for me!

Anal Play
We briefly touched on vibrators for anal play above. Any standard vibrator can be used for anal play; just make sure you wash them before inserting them into your pussy again. Additionally, with any type of anal play, you will need to make sure you use a *lot* of lubricant, and that you start out slow; if something is hurting, you need to stop and reassess. You may not be relaxed enough, it may be happening too fast, or you may need more lube. If it is something you don't want to do, then take a pass on it for now.

Butt Plugs

Butt plugs are great for experimenting with anal play, and can allow you to explore this realm safely. They come in several different sizes, are often made of silicone, glass, or metal, and have a flared base that prevents them from slipping up in there and getting lost. The base usually comes in a T-bar, which, for a butt, is more comfortable; however, there is also a rounded base that is often used for more decorative purposes. It is generally recommended that a plug is tapered, allowing a gentler approach to penetration. When applied correctly, they can be awesome for stimulating the ring of nerves around the anus.

The majority of people want to know want to know which anal toy they should pick. The vibrator or dildo is considered to me more of a dynamic toy, used for the in-and-out sensations that simulate anal sex. A butt plug is inserted and will usually stay in place, allowing for a full sensation. These can even stay in during day-to-day activities. There are also plenty of options for butt plug starter packs; these usually have a couple of different sizes, so you can work your way up in size. Some also come with lube; others with an enema bulb, which help to clean the area beforehand.

Anal Beads

Anal beads are made up of multiple spheres or balls that are either connected via string or molded as a single, flexible unit. They should have a larger ring or stopper at the end to prevent them from getting lost, as well as to promote easy removal. Oftentimes, the beads will be different sizes, which can increase pleasure during use. They are used to provide pleasure both during the insertion and removal of the beads. I would suggest getting some made of silicone due to the ease at which you can clean and sterilize them, in addition to their being non-porous yet flexible.

The insertion and removal of these beads in and out of the anus can provide pleasure. If you are new to anal play, I would suggest starting out with smaller beads and working your way up to provide the most sensation. People are oftentimes concerned about how they will feel after insertion, but most of the time, their main effect occurs with insertion and removal. It should not be uncomfortable.

Anal beads are great for solo play or with a partner, and are typically used either as foreplay or in pursuit of orgasm. As always, make sure you use lots of lube to prevent any discomfort, and practice deep, controlled breaths. During foreplay, after lubrication, you can gently insert beads, one by one, for stimulation. This can be done alone, or with some masturbation on the rest of your genitals. It works great for building anticipation and pleasure, and, generally speaking, you can leave them there throughout your sexual encounter. This can add a delicious layer of stimulation, although it is important to note that you should not experience any discomfort while they are there. To remove them, there are two options that are most common: removing them slowly as you build closer and closer to orgasm; and removing them a bit faster during your actual orgasm, thus getting full genital stimulation and an orgasm, all at once. This can create a whole new experience or orgasm!

Prostate Massagers

Prostate massagers are designed for men to stimulate—you guessed it—the prostate. Massaging the prostate can give a man a glorious, full-body orgasm, with or without ejaculation. Men who are open to the idea of prostate massages open a whole new realm of orgasm and sensations that they would not have access to otherwise. Much like the G-spot wands for women, prostate massagers are super effective due to their design, possessing a precise curvature and pressure made for stimulating the prostate. It is usually fairly slender, and has a base so as to prevent losing it up the rectum. This is also designed to stimulate the prostate through the perineum. These can also come with a vibrating option, or, alternatively, you can choose one just for insertion. Most of these also have a remote-control option. Prostate massagers are great for anyone who does not want to get "hands-on" when massaging the prostate. The Lelo brand, in my opinion, is the leader of this market.

Nipple Toys

The nipples provide you with an option for additional stimulation during sex, and can even supply a new kind of orgasm (more on that in a bit). One of your first points of consideration before engaging in nipple play, however, is do you even like your nipples being stimulated? I'm talking about having them sucked on, pinched, or maybe a little nibble. If not, then this may not be your thing; but if you do, then there's is an array of items that can be used for nipple play. The first option is to use the ever-so-versatile vibrator. You can literally stimulate your nipples by just touching them with this go-to toy. This usually works well once the nips are already warmed up and ready for some action—or you can even use a glass or metal dildo to provide a cold sensation across the nipples. But what else is there?

Nipple Clamps

People are often afraid of nipple clamps for fear that they will hurt; however, one of the key features in most clamps is having a screw or clamp so you can adjust how much pressure is being applied. This can feel as light as someone squeezing your nipples with their fingers, increasing as pleasure dictates. The whole preface of clamp-related pleasure is that it occurs via blood getting trapped in the tissue, making them super sensitive to the touch. Something to consider when purchasing is whether the clamps have a protective rubber covering or not; the ones without are for those who are probably more advanced, so if you are just starting out, I would definitely get one with a protective rubber end to reduce the amount of discomfort experienced.

You can also get them as either individual clamps, or attached with a chain to add some weight for sensation. There are even nipple clamps that come with vibrating attachments. There is no wrong or right!

To use a nipple clamp, you can either place it directly on the end of the nipple for more immediate stimulation, or you can start be placing it further back towards the areola so as to reduce overstimulation. Don't allow the clamp to close suddenly; make sure it is controlled, or it may be uncomfortable. Start with it at the least pressure and increase as desired. Many also find it pleasurable to have your nipples gently sucked on when placing them, or with them on. Leave them on as long as it feels good. To remove, simply take them off by opening the clamp—or, for those with more experience (or who like BDSM) may choose to pull them off, which can allow for a sudden sensation that can be pleasurable.

If you are afraid of clamps but are intrigued by the sensation, you have another option: nipple suckers. Also known as "pumps" or "vacuums", these toys can feel like mouths on the nipples; so, if you like that sensation but don't have a partner, these are a good way to go. You can apply them and leave your hands free for masturbation. They work in the same as clamps by gently increasing the blood flow with their strong suction, allowing for additional sensation.

Kink

BDSM and kink is a whole other realm in and of itself, and deserves its own book (which, by the way, there are plenty of). "BDSM" stands for Bondage and Discipline, Dominance and Submission, Sadism and Masochism— but there is nothing that states you have to participate in *all* of these aspects to enjoy it. Don't like bondage? Don't do it. Not sure if you want to be submissive? No problem. There is only one hard and fast rule when it comes to kink...

Everything is consensual.

These types of relationships are all about an erotic power exchange, agreed upon by both partners—not one person having power over the other. Boundaries are set, and everything is pre-negotiated. Remember, there is nothing that says you have to be tied up and gagged (unless you want to be); for you, kink can include something as nipple clamps, which we just discussed. Nipple clamps are actually a nice way to start to move from vanilla sex towards BDSM; and, indeed, several of the toys/products used in kink can produce a lot of pleasure when used correctly. If you are curious about it, make sure you do some research to allow for safe play, and make sure your partner is willing to explore this aspect with you. The three words that are most valued in this realm are Safe, Sane, and Consensual. Safety and consent should always be top priority—no exceptions.

What Now?

Now that we have covered some of the basic toys, it is now up to you to use them in masturbation, partnered sex, or both. The next question may concern how you can approach adding them to the mix with your partner, and, depending on your relationship, this can be either really awkward, or super-easy.

The first thing you need to do is talk about it. Unless you have already had a conversation about toys in some form, I do not recommend whipping out a vibrator in the middle of sex; have that conversation beforehand. If your partner is a little unsure about the whole concept, it may help to reassure them that adding a toy is in no way a reflection of their abilities, but that it is a great way for couples to increase intimacy, thereby allowing them to explore their sexuality and intimacy on a deeper level. In fact, using a toy with a partner can mean that there is a certain level of comfort within the relationship that may not be present in those where toys aren't used.

Finally, you have to be honest! Talk about why you want to add toys to the mix: if it is part of your personal Sex Goddess journey, then say that; or, alternatively, it may be that you want something new and exciting, especially if you have been with the person for a substantial amount of time. As humans, we crave novelty, and by experiencing it together, you can reinforce your relationship to something even stronger than before. Saying that, if something is just an absolute hard no, then be honest about that as well; you may be okay with a vibrator but not anal toys.

Once you have had such a conversation and both parties are willing, I recommend shopping together for new toys. Make sure you don't step over any boundaries that were agreed upon. You can either go to an adult novelty store, or, if you are too shy (or don't have one nearby), you can shop online together. A good option to get a good evaluation of toys is to host a Pure Romance or Passion Party, or something of the like. Invite your tribe over, have a few drinks, and make a fun night of having different toys presented to you by a well-educated individual who can explain each option. After the main party is over, you and your partner can pick what suits you best whilst receiving a discount for hosting the gathering. It's a win-win situation.

SEX GODDESS ACTIVITY

Please turn to Page 38 of your Sex Goddess Workbook now and complete **Challenges 1-3**.

CHAPTER 16:
PARTNER CONNECTIONS

Sex is more than an act of pleasure, it's the ability to be able to feel so close to a person, so connected, so comfortable that it's almost breathtaking to the point you feel you can't take it. And at this moment you're a part of them.

—Thom York

THE ABILITY TO CONNECT with a partner *intimately* via shared sexual energy is a sacred gift. Each time we engage a person in this type of experience, we share a part of our soul with them, and they with us. This goes beyond having sex; we can have sex with anyone, after all. I am talking about the willingness to be vulnerable, open, honest, deliberate, and raw with another human being, in an experience that can allow us to transcend our personalities and delve directly into our souls in a more profound way than what we ever thought was possible.

It is a process that requires patience and a readiness to trust another person. Both partners must be of a willing nature when it comes to understanding the full experience: there should be no fear, coercion, or regret. It is okay to be nervous when trying something new, but you should never feel like you have to do something you don't want to do, and nor should your partner.

Connecting in this way comes easily for some, whilst others may find they have to work to relinquish control and accept vulnerability. The funny thing here is that these two people are usually the ones who ae most drawn to each other; they tend to balance each other out whilst simultaneously being on opposite spectrums. This is where you have to learn how to communicate well with your partner about your desires, wants, fears, and limitations. It is about learning these subtle things about one another that others don't see. Knowing your partner inside and out (literally) allows you to more easily attain ecstasy; you feel safe, which allows you to drop your guard completely and be open.

As we move onto the subsequent chapters (comprised of more techniques teaching ways of attaining physical pleasure), I think it is important that we first start with your connecting with your partner on a more spiritual level. You may be rolling your eyes at me right now, and that's okay; as long as you are willing to give it a go. I'm not asking you to go to church together; rather, I want you both to participate in a few exercises, designed to open the flow of energy between the two of you prior to ever becoming sexual. You may feel it's a bit of a woo-woo type of experiment, and that's okay, too. Regardless, I encourage you to complete the challenges; they are awesome, and do, in fact, set the tone for what's next.

SEX GODDESS ACTIVITY

Please turn to Page 41 of your Sex Goddess Workbook now and complete **Challenges 1-2**.

CHAPTER 17:
THE EROTIC MASSAGE

Touch me, touch the palm of your hand to my body as I pass,
Be not afraid of my body.

—Walt Whitman, Leaves of Grass

Many lovers are 'off to the races': Hurtling towards orgasm,
they miss the excitement of sensual meanderings along
the way.

—Alexandra Katehakis, Mirror of Intimacy: Daily
Reflections on Emotional and Erotic Intelligence

THE EROTIC MASSAGE IS the slow, purposeful act of sensually massaging your partner. Done correctly, it also presents the opportunity to experience ecstasy. It is often pleasurable for both the giver and the receiver, and can be done as an individual sexual act or as a form of foreplay before intercourse. It has many potential variations, each presenting a unique experience. The erotic massage can be simple and focused in on one area, such as the breasts, or may be slow, centering on the extended exploration of the body in its entirety. It awakens deep-rooted sexual energy that has been concealed within you, waiting to be released. The goal of the Sex Goddess is to encourage the flow of sexual energy, leading to ecstasy—for themselves or their partner.

There are many goals of the erotic massage, and, of course they differ between each couple. You may be hoping to use it as a means to help relax prior to sex—to become open to the possibilities, shift any chatter from your mind, slow down, and explore the body more intricately. It can help you to identify new erogenous zones, as well as to activate them so that you have a more sensual, ecstatic experience. It can also be helpful in taking your sexual energy deeper as you submit to the extended slow discovery of your body's desires, listening to the nonverbal communication of anticipation-filled breathing and moans, as well as witnessing the undulations of pleasure experienced throughout the body via different types of sensual tactile stimulation.

The erotic massage can be spontaneous or a detailed, planned adventure. If you have never participated in the erotic massage with your partner, it may be best to communicate about it, if you intend for it to be such an extended experience: speak of the exploration of one another's bodies, and determine if there is anything that would not okay during such an act. Voice what you want to achieve from the experience, as well as what the expected outcome(s) may be, if any. Understand and respect the limits of your partner. Simple, spontaneous, and focused erotic massages, such as those directed toward the neck or feet, are often okay to do without a big discussion beforehand. Read your partner's cues from body language and ask them how it feels; good communication is key in keeping the flow of sexual intimacy going. The erotic massage is about awakening sexual energy; there is no need to know how to use professional techniques (e.g., shiatsu techniques; deep tissue techniques; Swedish techniques). As long as it feels good, then go with it.

Types of Touch

Knowing and understanding the different types of touch can be imperative when performing an erotic massage. Whilst each has its own value and contribution to the erotic massage, your partner may not necessarily like the sensation each of them produces. It is important to learn each one, as well as where to use them on the body and at what time during the erotic massage. There is no one correct approach to this: people experience different sensations and levels of intensity for each of their erogenous zones. Ask them what feels the best.

Here are some of the most common touch techniques used in the erotic massage.

1. **Featherlight.** This touch is just as it sounds: it is very soft and light on the skin, creating a very sensual tactile stimulation. It is good for at the very beginning or end of the erotic massage, and can also be used on extremely sensitive areas, such as the clitoris, to help increase anticipation.

2. **Stroking.** This is a repetitive touch, going in the same motion over the same body part repeatedly. It can be a light or firm touch, and can be done on any body part with ease.

3. **Rubbing.** This is a deeper, firmer touch that can increase blood flow. It is more often done on a larger muscle or body part, such as the back, thighs, or buttocks. When done more gently, it can also be used on the breast, or other areas with softer tissue.

4. **Percussion.** This includes tapping, spanking, tickling, and/or repetitive cupping, and can be used at different intensities, from soft to hard. Make sure it is okay with your partner to use this technique, and establish what intensity they would prefer.

5. **Scratching.** This uses the ends of your fingernails, and can be very erotic when done lightly. Usually done on thicker skin, such as the back, shoulders, or buttocks, the intensity may increase with arousal if your partner is enjoying it.

6. **Kneading.** This technique is usually done with your knuckles, the ball of your hand, or even with your forearm. It is a deeper, more intense massage, and has the potential to be more painful to some. Watch your partner's body language, or ask them if it is too much, or if they would like it harder. This technique is designed for the larger muscles of the body.

7. **Pinching.** This stimulation may not be for everyone; its use at the right time and with the right intensity is key. I would advise using this technique later during the erotic massage. It may be used on earlobes, lips, nipples, fingers, toes, and the labia. It usually does not require a lot of pressure, so start low and work up from there. Don't go in directly with this technique on any body part.

8. **Manipulation.** This technique is used to flex and bend wrists, elbows, knees, hips, and ankles. It is good for relaxing your partner earlier during the massage. Ensure your partner doesn't have any

joint-related issues or any pain when using this technique.

In addition to the types of touch discussed above, we have to consider the variations that go along with any erotic massage. These include, but are not limited to:

- Rhythm;
- Pressure;
- Tempo;
- Pace;
- Location;
- Sequence;
- Direction;
- Duration;
- Intention;
- Sides.

These variations in touch can greatly add to or diminish the amount of pleasure your partner receives; hence, we must be mindful of how we are touching our partner so as to ensure maximum pleasure. Make sure to watch out for verbal clues (e.g., direct comments; moans), as well as nonverbal clues (e.g., muscle tightening; grimacing; strained breathing; open body language). If all else fails, ask them how what you are doing feels, and what they want more or less of. Take time during the erotic massage to explore your partner's erogenous zones.

An "erogenous zone" is defined as "an area of the body that is more prone to stimulation and has an increased sensitivity when stimulated, leading to sexual response, sexual arousal, fantasies, and, potentially, orgasms". Erogenous zones vary between individuals, and each person has a preference in regard to the pressure and intensity of the massage. This is often dependent on the concentration of nerve endings in each zone. Engaging a person's erogenous zones qualifies as an act of intimacy, and can be done either independently or as a precursor to intercourse.

The common erogenous zones include the:

- Neck;
- Collarbone;
- Ears;
- Lips;
- Forehead (or "Third Eye");
- Sternum;
- Breasts;
- Nipples;
- Navel;
- Lower back;
- Inner thighs;

- Perineum;
- Vulva;
- Clitoris;
- Anus;
- Scrotum;
- Penis;
- Fingers;
- Hips;
- Buttocks;
- Feet;
- Toes.

The list can go on, but is not always all-inclusive; any place that is a turn-on if gently kissed or massaged can be classified as an erogenous zone. Think about how your partner has responded to the previous stimulation of these areas, and make it a goal to seek these different areas, erotically exploring them with different sensations, touches, and rhythms. If you have never touched each of the erogenous zones, take time to slowly caress each area during your erotic massage. Watch and listen to how your partner responds.

Now that we have reviewed the different kinds of touch, we need to prepare the setting and ambiance. Setting the space is an intricate part of any type of massage—at least if it's going to be a good one.

Set Up Your Space

The first step is to create a sacred space for the experience. Remove distractions such as cell phones (turn on the Do Not Disturb feature) and the TV. If you have children, make sure they are in bed—or, better yet, get a babysitter. I love it when couples "go away" for the night down the road at a beautiful hotel with no disruptions.

The giving partner should assist in building a comfortable nest for the receiving person: choose a room with a comfortable temperature, pillows, and soft lighting. It is important to ensure that the giving partner is in a comfortable position, too. There is no wrong place to do an erotic massage: it can be on the bed, on the floor, or at a hotel getaway. As long as you both are happy and comfortable, anything works. You can have soft music if you desire, but is not required. Make sure you have a good-quality massage oil that is pussy friendly. I would also keep a towel handy. Set these items up to be within reach of your space.

Set Intentions

After everything in your space is ready, sit with your partner and practice soul gazing—no talking! You can hold hands, gently stroke one another's faces, or just quietly and be in the moment. Gaze upon one another in

THE SEX GODDESS DIARIES

love and light. Think about what you love about the person you are with, right here After the minute is up, the person receiving the massage should disclose their intentions: are they hoping to experience ecstasy, or maybe familiarize themselves with your sexual energy? Are they hoping to edge out of their comfort zone? Let your partner know of any fears or desires *you* may have, too. Now is the time to make any special requests or limitations. Be clear. Tell your partner that you appreciate them.

Request an erotic and sensual massage to be given freely and with desire; then, it is the giver's turn to express any intentions, desires, or fears. Speak freely and openly to one another. If the receiver has not removed any clothing, now is the time to do so. The giver may either remove their clothes also or keep some on, depending on the intentions at play.

The Erotic Massage

Before you even begin the massage, it is essential to remember the importance of your breathwork and to integrate this into the massage. If need be, you can refer back to Chapter 7 for review. The receiving partner can choose which body parts are attended to in the erotic massage. Start wherever they indicate as being the most desirable; this can be the back, breasts, abdomen…

There is no wrong or right. It can even change each time you perform the erotic massage, which is something I would actually suggest doing so as to keep the entire process novel and exciting. For this teaching, have your partner lay face-down so you can start at the back. Provide a simple cover sheet if necessary to make your partner more comfortable. Lights should already be dimmed, and, if preferred, have some incense/diffusers/candles and music, all supplies and props within arm's reach for adjusting, if wished.

Start with your massage oil; two tablespoons should be plenty to start with. Pour the oil into your hands, rub them together to ensure they are at the proper temperature, and glide prior to touching your partner. Gently place your hands on the middle of your lover's back and slowly let them descend down to their lower back. Glide your hands all the way back up to the tops of the shoulders and over to the neck, and back down.

Repeat each motion around six times on any part of the body. Be attentive for any feedback your partner has, and ensure that you are not applying too much pressure to your partner if this is uncomfortable for them. Remember that this is about pleasure, not working out deep fascia knots!

The Back

Repeatedly work your hands over their entire backside, gently stroking your hands over the buttocks and gliding them up onto the back again. You are now wakening the skin's sensations. Begin with featherlight touching and transition into strokes, progressively adding slight pressure and intensity. You can add gentle kisses anywhere along the way during this massage. Some gently kneading may also be pleasurable on this area; it is whatever feels good to your partner. Be sure to focus on the back and buttocks area for at least 5-7 minutes, as this gives your lover time to relax more into the massage, as well as to explore some of the erogenous zones that may be there.

Some of the more common erogenous areas include the lower back, the upper back, mid-spine, between the shoulder blades, and, of course, the neck. Typically, the curve of the butt at the top of the thigh is also an effective one. The fleshy parts of the body, such as the buttock, can handle more pressure. Try different techniques with more pressure: squeeze and rub the cheeks with progressively increasing firmness. Firm, fluid movements on the bottom can be very stimulating for your lover. Be mindful of tickling if your lover does not like it. You can incorporate some light scratching on the back, too; men particularly seem to enjoy this aspect. This can be done in long, fluid motions on the entire length of the back, or it may be done in circular patterns. Move to the lower back and apply pressure to the sacrum (the triangle at the base of spine). Be sure to press your hands on either side of the spine.

Be playful and spontaneous with your creativity. The mood of the massage can allow for different techniques: it may be a slow, deep, sensual touch requiring special attention to breathing and focused erogenous zones exploration; or it may be lighter and more whimsical, with giggling and playful erotic touch. As always, there is no right or wrong answer here.

Be sure you are engaging by listening to your partner's body language, and listen for sounds of pleasure, such as moans. Evaluate their breathing patters, and, as you start to explore their erogenous zones, ask your lover to say which ones they like the most and with which kind of touch. Keep your touch fluid, always keeping at least one hand on your partner at all times. You can tell them how much pleasure you derive from feeling their body in this aspect. Create sensual anticipation with small kisses or warm breath on the erogenous zones they have vocalized their heightened sensitivity in. Alter the types of touch you use to create more anticipation.

The Arms and Hands

Once you have built up your partners erotic fire on the back and buttocks, it is time to move to the arms and hands. In one fluid stroke from the back, choose one arm to go to, and move your hands from the neck, down the arm, all the way to the fingertips, and back up. You may want to start with some featherlight strokes up and down the whole arm a few times before starting back up at the shoulder with a firmer rub, both at the front and back. Work your way down the arm in this fashion. With each section of the arm, you may want to go back to some featherlight touches or stroking after the rubbing. Some people have erogenous zones on the back of their upper arms and don't even realize it. Place some gentle kisses here to see how your partner reacts.

Next, move down to the hand. Try using several different touches on the hands, and don't neglect each individual finger: make sure you slither your fingers in-between theirs at the webs. You can also do some oral play on the fingers, as this is a common erogenous area, when done with the correct kind of simulation.

After the hand massage, work your way back up the arm with more of a sensual featherlight touch. Without removing at least one hand, slide across the upper back to the other arm and do the same type of massage on that side that you just performed. Try to spend equal amounts of time on each side; always attend to both sides of the body equally.

The Lower Body

Once finished with the other arm, return your hands to your partner's back and perform a few sweeping rubs or featherlight touches up and down the length of the back a few times; then, do the same thing over the butt, to the lower body. Again, be mindful if your partner is ticklish.

Start by focusing on the back of the thigh. You can either be sitting off to the side of your lover, but I prefer to sit in-between their legs, as I find this position to be more intimate. You can initially do featherlight stokes on both thighs at the same time, or on each individual leg separately. Make sure you don't neglect the inner thighs, as this is a high erogenous zone for many. Do light, gentle touches up very close to the genitals, without actually touching them at this point. If you happen to graze the outer aspect of the genitals, that is okay, but it is not time to focus there. That time is coming!

After some gentle teasing and stroking, move to one leg. Start to incorporate firmer rubbing onto the larger muscle on the back of the thigh and work into kneading. At this point, you will be able to use your wrist or forearm to knead this area, providing a more relaxing sensation to the muscle whilst simultaneously providing some rest to your hands. It is a simple technique: roll the forearm up and down the back of the thigh like a rolling pin. The meatier the tissue, the more pressure you can apply. Whilst doing any of these techniques, you can apply gentle kisses or love bites to the buttocks, adding an additional kind of sensation to your partner.

Work your way down to the calf, starting by gently stroking the length of the calf before kneading this area, depending on how your lover likes it. Be sure to place some gentle kisses on the back of the thigh and knee, too. These areas are typically not good for gentle love bites, but ask your partner anyway.

Now work your ways down to the foot. The feet can be erogenous zones that provide high pleasure, yet are often less likely to be touched than other parts of the body. If your partner does not like their feet being touched, respect their feelings and only do what feels good to them.

Take one foot at a time and apply plenty of massage oil to it. Spread it around the ankle and onto the heel and toes. Use the palm of your hand to slide over the bottom of your partner's foot with firm pressure. Do this at least four times. This is also another area that can handle more of a deep kneading with the wrist or forearm; you can also rub the bottom of the foot with your thumbs whilst providing a stroking sensation to the top of the foot. Rotate the foot at the ankle both clockwise and counterclockwise and work down to the toes. Rub your forefinger between each toe, then gently pulling each toe away from the body. Rub each toe between two fingertips, ensuring you are bestowing as much attention to each toe as you would any other body part. Work your way back to rubbing the foot, back up the calf, to the thigh, onto the buttocks, and then land at the lower back. Use this as a starting point for the rest of the lower body. Ensure you spend about the same amount of time with the same intensity on both sides.

Once this side is done, work your way back up to the lower back once again and provide a few gentle strokes to the length of the back and neck.

Now, it's time for your lover to turn over! Hopefully you see a smile on your lover's face; after all, with the sensuality and relaxation your erotic massage is providing, who wouldn't be smiling?

The Front Side

Once your partner has turned over, give them a soft, sensual kiss. Lovingly caress their neck, collarbone, and shoulders, tracing these areas a few times, focusing mainly on the collarbone. Without touching their chest, work your way down onto the sternum, gently rubbing it or placing soft kisses there between the breasts and/or nipples. Work your hands from the sternum to the left collarbone and shoulder before working outwards, towards the arm. You can do many of the same motions that you did when they were on their back.

Work your way back up the arm and across the upper-chest, providing the same loving attention to the other arm. Play and explore the erogenous zones of the neck, collarbone, inner arms, and fingers. I know you are highly turned on right now, but one of the goals was to explore every inch of your lover, including their erogenous zones. Savoring this slow process continues to build sexual energy. Work your way back to the collarbone and sternum without touching the chest/breasts.

Awakening the Chest and Abdomen

As you are kissing and exploring the sternum, empty some more oil into your free hand and then place your hands over the belly button. In a slow and controlled fashion, rub from the belly button up the stomach and onto the chest/breasts, around the nipples, onto the sternum, and back down to the belly button.

Do not initially stimulate the nipple directly: focus on the abdomen and the breast tissue. You may ask you partner how they want this area to be rubbed. Do this several times; it is inciting due to its high level of sexual energy. It is sensual, and feels amazing! Enjoy watching your lover's face and hearing the sounds of pleasure they make as you do this. Remind them (and yourself!) of slow and controlled breathing. Male chests can handle a higher intensity of rubbing and stroking than most female breasts.

Listen to how your lover is responding and ask them how it feels and what they want more of. This should be one of the more erotic parts of the massage, so make it as pleasurable as possible.

Both men and women have a high amount of sensation in their nipples: for some, this is to such a high degree that even the slightest touch is almost overwhelming, whilst for others, this doesn't do much for them. With a gentle nipple massage, you and your partner can explore this erogenous zone. Do not rush through this part unless it is not pleasurable to your partner: make sure you are looking for feedback during the nipple massage, both verbal and nonverbal.

Place your hands gently over the nipples and rub them with the palm of your hands. You can do this one nipple at a time, or both at the same time. Now place the nipple between your thumb and your third finger and gently pull on it to elongate it ever-so-slightly. Do this slowly to give your partner time to explore the sensations. You can do this a couple of times and see how he/she responds to each time; then, take the nipple between the same fingers and gently start to roll it clockwise and then counterclockwise in a slow, controlled motion. You can add the tip of your second finger to the top of the nipple in a stationary position to add additional stimulation to the nipple as you rotate it. Always look for feedback when you stimulate the nipples. You may apply soft kisses, or even take the nipple into your mouth, providing a warm, moist sensation to the now-heightened sensitivity of the area.

When you release the nipple, move back into a gentle breast/chest massage in the same pattern as before, working back down to the belly button. Take time to slowly massage the entire abdomen in a gentle manner and work your way down to the hips, applying additional pressure. Place gentle kisses across the hips and lower abdomen. I know the instinct right now is to go to the genitals next, but you must wait; the goal is to make a more fluid ebb and flow of sensuality and heightened sexual response to make for a more spectacular ending.

The Lower Body
Now, I want you to move from the hips down to the lower body. You can do many of the same techniques on the legs that you did when your partner was on the opposite side. Do not neglect either leg, nor the inner

thighs and feet. Work these erogenous zones and do not rush. As you work your way back up the thighs, place a couple of gentle kisses around the genitals as you are massaging the hips and inner/upper thighs.

It is finally time for the pussy/penis massage, which each have their own dedicated chapters. These massages can be incorporated into a full massage with where we just ended, or can even be done as a single event, which is amazing when you have less time or energy available. As a reminder, you should use a water-based lubricant for any pussy massage. Are you ready? Then turn the page.

SEX GODDESS ACTIVITY

Please turn to Page 43 of your Sex Goddess Workbook now and complete **Challenges 1-3**.

CHAPTER 18:
THE PUSSY MASSAGE

As the witnessing deepens, you start becoming drunk with the divine. This is what is called ecstasy.

—Rajneesh

THE PUSSY IS THE portal to the Heavens. It holds sacred power that can allow an individual to transcend worlds. Its luxurious purr of erotic arousal is what we all crave: it is warm and comforting; exotic and plush; the center to all life. Men and women both are desirous of the pussy's divine power, each for their own purpose; each for their own pleasure. A pussy massage awakens the innate energy that is possessed by a woman and allows her to kindle that sexual power for different purposes.

The pussy massage is very erotic and a deeply awakening form of touch. When done correctly, it can ignite ecstasy that is lying dormant within any woman. It works heavenly to engulf yourself in sexual energy, and can even help you release negative energies from your past that have been binding you. It can be a spiritual, meditative, and restoring experience. It is transformative.

There are several names for it out there, the two most common being the "pussy massage" or "yoni massage". None of them are wrong, and all provide a beautiful experience. You can take what I am going to teach you and adjust it to whatever works best for you, but by learning the basics, you can experience a massage like no other. I would plan on doing this activity for at least 15 minutes (preferably 20-30 minutes). With a pussy massage, there is no expectation of intercourse to follow, unless you both choose to do so. I do recommend having a pussy massage without intercourse on a regular basis. The full experience requires a willingness in participation from both you and your partner; it is a joint effort in giving and receiving for a truly luxurious sensual massage. You must be willing to follow the steps required to attain the ecstasy we discussed in Chapter 6. Are you ready?

Set Up Your Space

This is the same as for the whole-body erotic massage. Please refer back to this section in the previous chapter before continuing.

Set Intentions

Again, this is the same as for the whole-body erotic massage. Please refer back to this section in the previous chapter before continuing.

Awaken the Breasts

Note: If you are continuing from the full-body massage skip down to the next section.

Get into a comfortable position using any of the pillows, blankets, etc. that you set up before. The giver should place a hand over the receiver's heart for a moment whilst she starts to breathe. Start by awakening and moving your energy with circular breathwork. An even flow of breathwork should be continued for at least 10 minutes allowing any sexual energy to flow through it. Once you have connected with their heartbeat, gently start to massage the breasts: tart by circling the outer edges of them with your fingers and working your way towards the center. Don't immediately go for the nipples: concentrate on the feel of the breasts. Caress them using your palms, keeping your hands flowing. After a few minutes, use three fingers to gently rub the nipples in circular motions so as to awaken them. Remember to encourage her to keep breathing properly. Apply some massage oil, ensuring if it is cool to warm it in your hands before touching her (unless this temperature is what is desired). Using your entire hands, massage both breasts simultaneously. Rub your hands up onto her chest and then down her breastbone, then back up, circling back to the breasts. Do this a few times, and, as you go down the breastbone, keep swooping your hands down onto her tummy, then out to her hips.

Awaken the Pelvis

Move from her hips to her outer thighs and over to her inner thighs. Gently (but firmly enough to not tickle), rub the groin area and progress to her lower abdomen. Massage in a circular pattern over where you imagine her uterus to be and join your hands together, sliding them back up to the breastbone. Start the pattern over again, repeating this at least three times. On the third round, move one hand back over her heart, and keep one over her lower abdomen. Pause there for a moment and connect your breathing together; it should be rhythmic in nature. Bring both hands back to center over her lower abdomen, massaging it in a circular motion using your palms.

The Vulva Massage

Awaken The Pussy. Place the heel of your palm over her mons pubis and gently cup the vulva with you hand.

Breathe and emit sexual energy into this amazing pussy with gratitude. Hold it there for just a few moments; this grounds the energy to her. Make sure you are both continuing proper breathing and that the receiving partner is a comfortable position (I like to place pillows under knees, which allows for more focus on the massage and less on the position of my legs). With your whole hand, begin to gently rub the pussy in small circular motions, allowing the vulva to awaken. With the tips of your three middle fingers, gently massage the perineum for a few strokes before going back to circular massage over the whole pussy. Alternate between these a few times.

Labia Love. After finishing the stroke on her perineum, take two of your fingers, and, with some pressure, rub them up and down the outer area of the labia majora, up and down. Watch how the lips start to spread as they become aroused, offering the deliciousness of what lays beneath. After several passes of two-finger labia love, use a third middle finger to gently stroke just inside the labia as your other fingers continue to stroke the outer area. Feel her wetness. You can go back to circular pussy awakening and then back to labia love at any point during this massage.

Tapping Into Pleasure. With the same three fingertips, begin to lightly tap all over her pussy. If her clit is engorged, gently tap it a few times before continuing to tap the entire vulva. Move up and down her pussy, allowing this sensation to build excitement in her clit. Don't apply continuous simulation to her clit, as we want to build her excitement up and let it edge back down.

Mound Around. With the palm of your hand, apply a slight pressure over her clit and rub in a slow, circular motion. Make sure you are not applying too much pressure.

I recommend doing these in order first and then alternating in any way that is pleasurable to your partner. The key is to make sure both your breathing is controlled and that the concept of edging that was taught in the masturbation section is employed, allowing orgasmic energy to build.

The Clit Massage

New Moon. After the vulva massage, gently push the mons pubis up with one hand. The clit is hopefully already engorged and is easily identifiable. Using two fingers, start to do a New Moon shape around the clit. This will be similar to the orbiting technique we learned in the masturbation chapter. Keeping the clitoral hood over the glans, circle your fingers from one side, over the top, to the other side, without directly touching the glans.

Figure-Eight. Without stopping, transition from a New Moon to tracing a figure-eight pattern over the clit, keeping the hood in place. Do this at least three times, and, from there, you can continue the patterns New Moon circles or figure-eights whilst occasionally exposing the clit from under the hood and gliding across it in the process. Just because the clit may be exposed now does not mean we should bombard it; continue a circular flow to and from it, allowing for small breaks of direct stimulation.

Direct Hit. Gently push the clitoral hood back and expose the clit glans; hopefully, it is throbbing in anticipation. This is where you can repeatedly encircle the happy clit with your thumb or pointer finger. Remember to allow her to edge close to climax and then, using a grounding gesture of holding your hand over her vulva, allow her to return from the brink or orgasm. If need be, remove your hand from her vulva and place it on her lower abdomen to allow the sexual energy to ebb down.

The amount of pressure applied to each of these variations is going to be down to personal preference, so ensure you are communicating with one another the whole time.

The Internal Massage

Open The Vault. Return for a moment to labia love, stroking her with three fingers, gently caressing the opening a few times; then, using two or three fingers, slowly inset your fingertips no more than two inches into her vagina. (Remember how many nerve endings are in the first few inches!) Start to move your fingers in a circular motion feeling all the edges of the vaginal opening. Return back to labia love and start the motions over again.

Hide-and-Go-Seek. After about three cycles of opening the vault, turn your palm towards the ceiling and take two of your fingers, inserting them inside her vagina and press *firmly* along the front of the vaginal wall (think tummy side). Begin to make a circular motion, making sure you are firm but not hurting, and feel for the G-spot. Many women can find this very pleasurable, but some have the sensation of needing to urinate. This is most likely due to the stimulation of the Skene's Glands (remember our anatomy lesson). Stroke this area as much as she likes.

Donut Shop. Here we will look for the cervix. Remember I said it will feel like a firm donut? Using the same fingers, reach deeper into her vagina. Don't thrust it; search gently. Feel for a firm object. If you find it, begin stroking it. It will be easiest to do this in a circular pattern. If you hit it too hard when looking for it, she will most likely tell you.

Dual Massage

A dual massage is just a matter of incorporating the breast, clitoral, and internal vaginal massages. Communicate with one another and start to build more and more orgasmic energy. You can use a combination of any of the techniques in pursuit of achieving ecstasy. Use the orgasmic breathwork that we learned in Chapter 7 to strengthen and inspire the impending climax. Allow your partner to be in the moment and take in her beauty as she revels in your gift to her. Encourage noise and rhythmic hip undulations as she releases to the Gods.

Recovery

Slowly remove your fingers from her vagina and place you hand in a grounding position over her pussy, feeling the energy emanating from it. If she likes gentle breast stimulation during this time, you can continue to do so. Rub your hands over her thighs and hips; kiss and gently massage her lower abdomen over her womb and just sit by her, not touching unless she asks you to. She will most likely need a few, or possibly even several, minutes to recover.

Be quiet and let her revel in the afterglow of the ecstasy you have gifted her. Do not be alarmed if there are giggles or tears, or if she lays there, quiet, with her eyes closed. Each of these reactions are normal, and can differ each time. The sexual energy that was just felt can sometimes be overwhelming. When she is ready, help her sit up and get her a glass of water for her to drink.

Once she is recovered, show gratitude towards one another. If the pussy massage was done correctly, you will know with certainty that she enjoyed it, and you will not need to press for validation. Tell her how beautiful she was to watch during the experience.

SEX GODDESS ACTIVITY

Please turn to Page 46 of your Sex Goddess Workbook now and complete **Challenges 1-5**.

CHAPTER 19:
THE PENIS MASSAGE

We tend to think of the erotic as an easy, tantalizing sexual arousal. I speak of the erotic as the deepest life force, a force which moves us toward living in a fundamental way.

—Audre Lorde

THE LINGAM MASSAGE, OR penis massage, is an erotic and sensual massage that rivals the pussy massage, going way beyond a simple hand job; it is meant as a purposeful, divine source or pleasure, as well as to withhold immediate ejaculation. Whilst this is not always what men want to hear, men can, in fact, reach a deeper, more cosmic, whole-body orgasm by doing so; they just have to be willing to sit back, be patient, and revel what you are offering. This is difficult for many men whose goal for so many years has been the moment of ejaculation, so don't be surprised if you face some resistance after making such a suggestion.

The purpose of the penis massage is to build sexual energy in a man in a way that he has never experienced before. It can sometimes be overwhelming when first starting, and if it is, that's okay; perfection is not a requirement, but by learning the basics, you can ultimately provide your partner with an experience like no other. I would plan on doing this activity for at least 15 minutes (preferably 20-30 minutes). As with the pussy massage, there is no expectation of intercourse to follow, unless you both choose to do so. It is beneficial to have regular penis massages to help circulate the man's energy in a way that they do not often get to do. The full experience requires a willingness in participation from both you and your partner; it is a joint effort in giving and receiving. He should also be willing to follow the steps required to attain ecstasy that we discussed in Chapter 6. Are you ready?

Set Your Space
This is the same as for the whole-body erotic massage. Please refer back to this section in the previous chapter before continuing.

Set Intentions
This is the same as for the whole-body erotic massage. Please refer back to this section in the previous chapter before continuing.

Awaken the Chest

Note: If you are continuing from the full-body massage, move onto the next section.

Have your partner get into a comfortable position in the space you have set up. Place a hand over the receiver's heart for a moment whilst he starts to regulate his breathing. Encourage your partner to partake in circular breathwork. If he is unfamiliar with it, instruct him on how to use his breath and do it with him. An even flow of breathwork should be continued for at least 10 minutes, allowing any sexual energy to flow through it. Once he has established his breathing and you have connected with his heart, you can start the massage.

Begin by taking one or both of your hands, and, just with your fingertips, very softly start to do circular motions over his chest. If he has chest hair, do it just on the hair; if he does not, do so ever-so-lightly on his skin. You can move to his neck or shoulders later; focus on the chest for now. We tend to want to go directly for the cock too often, so concentrate instead on stirring sexual energy throughout his body. You can start to add a little more pressure to the circular motions and move from his chest to his neck, then returning to his chest. After you have done this a few times, go ahead and, with just your fingertips, start this pattern on his abdomen. Gently stroke your fingers all the way down to his lower abdomen, again avoiding touching his cock. Build the anticipation: circle back up to his chest and encircle his nipples with one finger, either one at a time or both together. As you do this, you can gently nuzzle his chest or abdomen, providing a warm sensation with your breath and perhaps giving it a few soft kisses.

Awaken the Pelvis

Begin to move your hands to his hips and outer thighs and then over to his inner thighs. Gently return your hands to the tops of his thighs, and, with the palms of your hands, rub up the thighs, up over his hips, and to his lower abdomen, where your hands can meet; then, travel back down to the starting point, taking care to massage the area surrounding his cock but avoiding direct contact so as to build the excitement and anticipation.

After doing this at least three times (you can always do more, if you wish), move one hand back up over his chest to cover his heart, and, with the other hand, ever-so-lightly cup his scrotum. Feel the sexual energy flowing between your two points of contact. Pause there for a moment and connect your breathing together; it should be rhythmic in nature. Bring both hands back and place your palms over his hips or thighs.

Penis Massage

There are several different strokes that we will be going over, and I encourage you to try each of them at least once. Find what your partner likes best, and don't you be shy about it, either! Penises can handle a lot, so be firm. Ask him to communicate with you in how it feels; if he wants the pressure to be harder or softer, he needs to tell you. Don't take it personally, and listen to his requests. Remember to maintain breathing as well. Ready?

Get your massage oil or lube and warm it between your hands, applying plenty of it to his cock, balls, and perineum. Gently place one hand on the shaft of the penis and stroke it in a controlled, up-and-down motion whilst gently fondling the scrotum with the other hand. Do this for about 2-3 minutes prior to initiating any of the following strokes.

The Healing Stroke. With the healing stroke, take the palm side of one of your hands and rub the underneath of the penile shaft. Do not wrap your hand around the shaft; keep it flat. Rub from the scrotum up to the head of the penis and back down again. Keep doing this pattern, either keeping a consistent speed or changing it up. This is also considered to be a transition stroke. Use this at any time when you are sequencing into another stroke technique.

Lemon Squeeze. Hold his cock with one hand around the shaft and, with your other hand, hold the tip of his dick in your palm and twist, as if you are squeezing the juice out of a lemon. You can do this at different speeds and intensities, directing your focus just to the "squeezing" hand or the "shaft hand" to gently stroke his cock as you perform the technique.

Making the Fire. Place the shaft of the penis between the palms of your hands, ensuring there are ample amounts of lubrication. Move one hand forwards and the other one backwards. Imagine his penis is a stick and you are trying to ignite a fire with this motion. Keep your hands flat as you do this motion. Start out slowly and increase the rhythm slowly.

Spiraling the Stalk. Take your thumb and first two fingers of each hand and wrap them around the penile shaft; now, twist each hand in a corkscrew motion over the penis, each going in the opposite direction of the other. You can do this down the entire length of the shaft with your hands right on top of each other, or you can do it with one had at the top just below the head of the penis and the other at the base of the shaft. You can also do this and work your way to have your hands meet in the middle. Do not go up onto the head of the penis or onto the scrotum with this technique, and make sure there is plenty of lubrication. Be sure to stay on his shaft.

_>

Wet and Wild. For this technique, concentrate of covering the head of the penis with your hands and sliding it down the entire length of the shaft with one hand right after another. Make it a fluid motion and repeat for about 10 strokes.

Million Dollar Point. With the Million Dollar Point, we will be focusing on his perineum (the space between his scrotum and his anus). Moving your fingers from his anus to his scrotum, feel for a small indention that is about the size of a pea. It is typically midway, but spend some time looking for the correct area. Once you find it, gently press inward with your thumb. This is called the Million Dollar Point in Taoism, and can elicit significant sexual stimulation. This is an external stimulation of the prostate gland, and can be very erotic. It should not hurt him, but feel quite pleasurable. You can stimulate the Million Dollar Point at any time during the penis massage.

Final Massage

A Final Massage is just a matter of incorporating the different strokes that are most pleasurable to him. Watch for all his verbal and nonverbal cues and start to build more and more orgasmic energy. The purpose, as with any type of massages, is to try and assist your lover in attaining ecstasy. Use the orgasmic breathwork that we learned in Chapter 7 to strengthen and inspire the impending climax. Allow your partner to be in the moment: bring his sexual energy to a higher level. The more you worked to build orgasmic energy by withholding climax during the massage, the stronger he will feel it during the moment of orgasmic release.

Encourage him to climax now and continue to stroke his Million Dollar Point as he does. Many men report experiencing full-body orgasms for the first time with this type of penis massage, as it allows for him to slow down and completely feel his body in the moment without the need of thinking about his performance. It truly is a gift to man.

Recovery

Place your hand in a grounding position over his cock or hips and feel the energy emanating from it. Rub your hands over his thighs and hips and place kisses on his lower abdomen; then, just sit by, not touching unless asked to do so. He may need a few minutes to a take it all in. Once he is recovered, show gratitude towards one another. Each of you should verbalize to the other what the most profound part of the process was for you.

SEX GODDESS ACTIVITY

Please turn to Page 51 of your Sex Goddess Workbook now and complete **Challenges 1-4**.

SECTION 4:
ORGASMS

CHAPTER 20:
THE ANATOMY OF AN ORGASM

*Orgasm is the involvement of the total body: mind, body, soul,
all together. You vibrate, your whole being vibrates, from the
toes to the head. You are no longer in control; existence has
taken possession of you and you don't know who you are.
It is like a madness, it is like a sleep, it is like meditation,
it is like death.*

—Osho

WHEN I SAY THE word orgasm, everyone always imagines the big climatic ending. It's something we all strive to have. Or at least I hope we all do. According to one study published in 2017, only 65% of straight women reach orgasm every time they have sex, whereas lesbian women are able to cum about 86% of the time. The difference being attributed to how women respond to their partner's needs, take more time, and understands their bodies better than their male counterparts. In comparison 95% of straight men reach orgasm each time with gay men cumming 89% of the time. I would love for these numbers to improve for everyone.

I know there are plenty of women out there who can fake it. I think one of my favorite movie scenes is from When Harry met Sally and actress Meg Ryan (Sally) is demonstrating how easy it is to fake an orgasm, doing it in the middle of a busy restaurant, to prove a point to her counterpart Harry who doesn't think a woman has ever faked it with him indicating that he could tell the difference. Sally sounds so convincing in her fake orgasm that she gains the attention of the entire place, everyone just staring at her with mouths gaping open. And after her very loud and authentic sounding orgasmic performance she then goes right back to eating her lunch like nothing happened, leaving everyone who was witness to her performance in awe while proving to her friend that he in fact could not tell the difference. The thing is, I don't want you to fake it! I want you to be able to experience an orgasm at will and as often as you like. Which leads me to my next question. How much do you understand orgasms?

Well get your nerd glasses back on, because we're going to go over the science of the orgasm. It's kind of like our anatomy lessons, I will try to keep it as straight forward and to the point as possible. But I firmly believe that if you don't understand something, you can't expect to get the effects and benefits from it. It's like wanting to drive a car but not knowing which pedal is the accelerator. Alright, got your nerd glasses on?

The sexual response is typically described as four parts. Arousal, Plateau, Orgasm and Resolution. After arousal begins the parasympathetic nerve process takes over causing the brain to send signals to increase blood flow to the genitals resulting in engorgement and lubrication in women, and erection in men. Your heart rate and breathing will increase and your body becomes awakened to the signals that are being sent back to your brain indicating pleasure. The central nervous system that controls sexual function becomes fully engaged and the brain starts to release large amounts of dopamine.

Dopamine is produced in the hypothalamus and is well established as the "reward" chemical in our brains. It is released when we do things that feel good such as having sex. High levels of dopamine results in the release of another brain chemical, norepinephrine, and the increased levels of this combination of juicy brain chemicals makes a person giddy, energetic, and often even euphoric. Sound familiar?

At the same time that your brain is getting flooded with dopamine and norepinephrine there are thousands of nerves that become awake and active during sexual arousal, triggered by the parasympathetic pathways, that are otherwise half asleep most of the time. Higher states of sexual arousal lead to more of these nerves being engaged, sending rapid signals back to the brain. Bottom line is the more aroused you are the more of your sexual nerves are activated leading up to the impending orgasm. These nerve signals that have been sent throughout the body at rapid speeds results in a wave of contractions of the pubococcygeus muscle, or PC muscle, which surrounds the vagina and the rectum. This muscle contraction is part of what is felt during orgasm in conjunction with a final surge of hormones.

The classic orgasm in women, most often seen with clit stimulation, last on average about 20 seconds (go team clit!) and there is rhythmic contraction of different muscles including the uterus, vagina, pelvic muscles and the anus. Those who have had a hysterectomy are still able to achieve climax despite not having a uterus anymore, thanks to all the other muscles and nerves that come into play. Women have the ability to be multi-orgasmic in the sense that they do not have a required amount of time, called a refractory period, before they can achieve their next orgasm. This means it can be back to back to back big O's for the ladies.

Men's orgasm on average last between 3-10 seconds and involve the anal sphincter, the prostate gland and the muscles around the penis to achieve ejaculation. Unlike women they do have a refractory period after ejaculation, which can last anywhere between several minutes to several hours, before they can achieve another orgasm. Now this doesn't mean they can't be multi-orgasmic at all. It is only after the refractory period starts when the man ejaculates. Men are capable of being multi-orgasmic though prostate orgasms.

The brain of both men and women have similarities and yet different processes during orgasm. And thanks to modern medicine we are able to understand the dynamics of what is actually happening in the brain during an orgasm.

With functional MRI's we can see a flood of dopamine and oxytocin in over 20 different regions of the brain. The dopamine gives of a sense of excitatory pleasure, which causes you to crave it again and again. Oxytocin is a hormone that initiates feeling of love and bonding. Using PET scans, we can see some similarity in both men's and women's brains. The portion of the brain that controls, reason, self-control and self-evaluation, shuts down and will decrease the fear and anxiety response. There is lower activity in the amygdala resulting in a trance like state that is often felt with and immediately after orgasm. This can reduce aggression in males and overall emotions in females. After this, a portion of the women's brains called the PAG (periaqueductal gray) stimulates the fight or flight response in women, explaining why so often they feel more awake and alive after sex, as compared to men who mostly just want to go to sleep. Following the orgasmic chemical response in the brain, our heart rates will return to normal and our muscles and brain activity will reach a more relaxed state.

I hope that wasn't too painful to read. If you ask me, I kinda like knowing how it all works. The more in tune you are with your body, the more natural and comfortable these experiences become.

The goal of The Sex Goddess is to be able to experience as many types of orgasms as often as she chooses. Yes, there are different types of orgasms, which we are going to cover in the upcoming chapters. I will teach you how to reach each delicious orgasm. Each of them has their own sensation and intensity. I do hope you work to experience each one individually so you learn to identify how each one feels. From there we can have a blended orgasm, which is a combination of two or more orgasms for a truly ecstatic experience.

SEX GODDESS ACTIVITY

Please turn to Page 56 of your Sex Goddess Workbook now and complete **Challenges 1-2**.

CHAPTER 21:
CERVICAL ORGASM

At the moment of orgasm you grow wings, defy gravity and your soul slips quietly across the universe like a shooting star."

—Chloe Thurlow

WHILE THE CLIT AND G-spot are the known hot spots to get a delicious orgasm, women must not forget about their other feminine pathways to pleasure. One that is overlooked: the cervix.

The cervix is most often looked at only as a structural component only in the female anatomy. When it is discussed, it is usually in the context of childbirth or at gynecologist visit. But if there is only one thing you have learned so far, I hope it's that nothing in the female body can escape from the sexual energy and power brewing in every one of us. The problem is that most often women don't understand the capabilities that their own body holds, both good and bad. What I mean by that is that although the cervix has the potential to provide pleasure, often it brings pain or discomfort, either through physical trauma such a pap smears, rough sex, child birth, or even through emotional trauma. When these experiences happen, the cervix may then become armored.

Did you just picture a little piece of hard armor covering your cervix? I did. And this is kind of what it's like. Any part of the human body that is exposed to trauma will pull back in a defensive mode and contract down and sheild itself. Think about if you were to burn your hand. Your hand instinctively recoils and clenches down from the pain. It's done before you have even had a chance to think about it. The next time your hand is near an open flame, its likely to automatically recoil in the same fashion even if it hasn't actually touched the flame. This is from a conditioning response that we all have that prevents us from experiencing further pain or injury. The same thing can happen with your cervix. It recoils, contracts down and can remain in a hypervigilant state of distress, causing it to become in a chronic state of contraction. This armored state can also be caused by emotional trauma as well, especially when that trauma is from our romantic relationships or sexual abuse. An armored cervix is often the cause of discomfort that women experience with sex when their cervix is stimulated.

So how does one learn how to de-armor her cervix? My suggestion is re-conditioning your body to understand that pleasure can exist in this lady part while learning how to have an orgasm with it. I'm sure right now you are probably like "what the heck is she talking about?" The cervix, when not contracted, has the ability to shower the body with immense waves of pleasure when stimulated correctly and can provide an intense full body orgasm. Now this is probably not gonna happen on the first try, or maybe even the thirtieth try. **But it can happen.** You must surrender yourself and be in the moment for this to happen.

Even if you achieve being able to feel your cervix on the first try it is going to be very difficult to convince it that what you're doing is pleasure if it is still in an armored state. The goal is to coax it into relaxation through repeated gentle physical stimulation while maintaining a state of mental relaxation. If you have previously experienced pain within the cervix, getting it to relax is going to be very hard to do, hence why it may take a while to achieve this goal. But I say let's give it a go. By de-armoring your cervix, you have the opportunity to not only explore a new realm of sexual pleasure, but also release physical and emotional trauma that is being held there.

Cervical Massage

Let's start working towards de-armoring the cervix by learning a gentle cervical massage. We're going to briefly go over how to reach your cervix again from the anatomy lessons. Before you ever begin to locate your cervix, start with soothing breathwork such as a Breath of Bliss. If need be review chapter 7 for these techniques. Remember to maintain your breath during this whole activity and remain in the moment. If you feel you are holding a significant amount of trauma in your cervix, I would recommend meditating for 10 minutes prior to any activity, and set some intentions for what you are trying to achieve.

To reach your cervix you will need to sit in a comfortable position like on the end of a bed, a toilet or in a squatting position (which I have found to be the best for my own exploration). It is going to be easiest to locate it when you are not ovulating or midcycle, or directly after sex, as the position of the cervix will change based on hormones and sexual arousal.

Once you have gotten into position, insert your index or middle finger deep into your vagina in somewhat of an upwards motion and feel for a slightly firm object amongst the soft give of the vagina. Your cervix can be deeper inside than you initially think, so if you don't feel it, don't despair. It may take several tries before you actually figure out where your cervix is. If you feel something firm and doesn't have much give, you have probably found it.

Remember there can be anatomical differences as well in women. Once you have located it, gently use your middle finger and trace circles over it. Continue breathing. If at any time it is painful, stop. If you have troubles reaching your cervix get help from a partner or use a dildo. I would not suggest a vibrator as we are trying to coax the cervix into relaxation not over stimulate it. Now there are a few techniques that can be done to help release tension and allow your cervix to become a source of pleasure. Let's go over them.

Slow Down

The first is to slow everything down. This should be a very purposeful experience. A slow hand from your partner (or your dildo) and slowing down your thoughts will go a long way. The cervix is like any other part of your body. If it is stimulated super-fast and hard over and over and over, without any slow and sensual warm up, it would be more aggravating than pleasurable. Allow the sensation to be deliberate and sensual. It doesn't matter if it is with a hand, cock or dildo. Keep it slow and intentional.

Holding Pattern

The second technique is called the "Holding Pattern". This is an important step so pay attention. Without thrusting of any kind (gentlemen are you reading this?) gently hold the cock/dildo against the cervix. This is going to take some effort and self-control for the men as they naturally want to thrust, but don't. Keep the cock in one place while holding her, breathing with her and looking into her eyes. Allow her body to relax into the cock or dildo. This may take several minutes. She will be able to tell you when she is ready for thrusting. Which leads to our next tip.

Thrust Properly

Remember when I said keep it slow and intentional? With either a cock or a dildo, do slow circular hip motions, allowing the tip of the cock to massage the cervix in a sustained rhythm. You can also do a little bumping action by very gently tapping the cervix with the end of the dildo or cock. This should not be a full force thrust though. Allow her to build pleasure at her pace. This may be holing the dildo in place and allowing her to do hip circles or thrust onto it, which also allow her control and power.

Maintain

The last technique is to maintain. After the woman has found which rhythm is most enjoyable, be consistent with it. Allow the cervix to be reconditioned with pleasure. The sensations will begin to build and she will become more open. Encourage her to feel bliss in her cervix and open herself to the possibility of a cervical orgasm. Remember this technique takes practice. Don't expect an orgasm the first time or even every time. When it does happen, it is important to know that this doesn't feel like the typical clit orgasm though. It often feels like waves of tingling or rumbling pleasure rolling throughout the body with a deep ecstatic release from the womb between the belly button and vagina. A woman's sounds may become more intense, almost guttural and raw sounding as she relinquishes herself to the depth of the moment.

Sounds amazing, right? Just remember, this orgasm can take quite a while to attain, but I encourage you to keep at it. When you continue to work towards the cervical orgasm, you allow sexual energy to flow more freely, releasing trauma, and allow your cervix to be reconditioned for pleasure. All good things.

SEX GODDESS ACTIVITY

Please turn to Page 58 of your Sex Goddess Workbook now and complete **Challenges 1-2**.

CHAPTER 22:
DEEP VAGINAL ORGASM

Within my body are all the sacred places of the
world and the most profound pilgrimage that I can ever
make is within my own body.

—Saraha

DEEP WITHIN A WOMAN there is a sacred space which is often unseen and unfelt, waiting to be provoked, providing an escape from reality. A connection of mind, body and soul for a ubiquitous divine experience that takes a woman beyond herself, even If only for a few moments. Too often it remains hidden, just as some of the greatest treasures and mysteries of this world usually do.

The deep reaches of the womb have potential that is too often forgotten, yet so vital to sexual energy, that we as women must learn to reclaim it. It is our right to feel the power within us. Hedonism is ready and waiting to be achieved through deep vaginal stimulation of the A-spot. It is a area of the body that is often unknown or misunderstood by many. As a Sex Goddess I want you to have the opportunity to seek the power within you, to wield a divine path through any orgasm of your choosing. So as with every other concept in this book, I am going to provide you with knowledge. How you use it is up to you.

The A-Spot

The A-spot, or the Anterior Fornix is located high on the front wall of the vagina, around 4-6 inches in from the vaginal opening, and a few inches higher than the G-spot, usually in front of the cervix. Let's go through step by step on how to find you're A-spot. You can try this on your own with fingers, dildo, vibrator or wand, or you can get your partner to help you out.

Start by finding inserting fingers or toy into your pussy a few inches, feeling for a patch of firm spongy tissue about the size of a walnut. This is your G-spot. Begin stroking it with one finger as if you were gesturing for someone to "come here". This should provoke some arousal and be sensual. It is definitely tempting to stay in this sweet spot, but our purpose right now is to go deeper.

I want you to push your fingers/toy about 2-3 inches further in, still focusing towards to front wall of the vagina. It has a softer spongy feeling, as compared to the firmer G-spot that you were just feeling. Now, instead of doing the same gesture that stimulates the G-spot, move your finger in a windshield wiper movement, back and forth across the area. Do not do an in and out motion. We are exploring right now, not fucking. Pay attention to the sensations. Again, some of the key aspects is maintaining your breathing and relax, be in the moment.

If you feel like you're just not getting it, try applying more pressure with your windshield movement, or go a little deeper. Research indicates that stimulating the A-spot can lead to more vaginal lubrication, so this may help you understand if you're in the right area. The A-spot is likely to cover a bit larger area, as opposed to the focused G-spot, which is why the windshield wiper method works well. Remember those thousands of nerve endings in the pelvis? Well there is a large number of those located in this area, which means there is a vast source of potential pleasure. At first it is probably not going to feel like when you stimulate the clit, or even the G-spot, but an entirely different, more sensual layer of pleasure.

So now that you have located your A-spot, what's the best way to experience an orgasm from it?

By going deep.

It is estimated that having *at least* 5 inches of fingers, toy or cock is needed, and depending on the woman's anatomy, possibly more. If you have done the exploration to find the A-spot, then you will be able to tell just how much you actually may need. Don't be shy about asking your partner to go deeper into you.

Angle

Exploring your A-spot and learning the best angle that provides pleasure is such an important part of this journey. So don't be shy about checking out the deep V out if this type of orgasm is one of your goals in becoming a Sex Goddess. Explore during different times for your cycle as well. Remember, the position of your uterus and cervix changes based on hormones and level of arousal. Therefore, the position of the cock/toy may need to change to avoid hitting the cervix and causing discomfort. The other thing that is usually needed to reach an A-Spot orgasm?

Consistency

Once you find the right angle and depth, there has to be consistency. It would be like hitting your clit two or three times and expecting an orgasm. Probably not gonna happen. Good steady DEEP stimulation is a key factor. No stop/start, change position, stop/start. Find what feels good and run with it!

There are a three favorite sex positions that can make finding this elusive area easier to locate. Often times the A-spot is naturally stimulated during a deeper fucking, the kind that leaves your legs weak. As far as which one is best? Well that's going to be up to you. Personal and physical comfort levels make a difference. Let's go over them.

Lifted Missionary

With this position you are in the missionary position, only you have a stack of pillows or blankets placed under your hips/ lower back while keeping your head on the bed. This allows your pelvis to be tilted in more of an upward position, providing more of a direct angle and approach to the A-spot during penetration. Be sure to go in gently at first to ensure that either the cock or toy is not going to be hitting the cervix and causing discomfort. Adjust your position until you feel pleasure. You can have your partner hold your legs up or you can tuck them towards your chest for a deeper penetration. This also allows for an easy access to the clit for a dual stimulation.

Cowgirl

C'mon my lovely Sex Goddess, it's time to get on and ride! The Cowgirl position allows for a deep penetration while giving you more control that the lifted missionary. You can decide the depth and speed with this position. To do this one, have you partner lay on their back, then straddle them with a leg on either side, and slide down onto the cock or dildo. Adjust your position, rock back and forth, lean front to back! Whatever it takes to locate you're A-spot! If you want to go a little deeper, change your leg position so that your feet are planted next to your partner, allowing your knees to pull closer to your chest, and have your partner do the thrusting, or you can bounce up and down. This position allows the Sex Goddess more power and control.

Doggy Style

This is another great position to hit the A-spot. Start out on all fours and have your partner enter your pussy from behind. Again, it may take some experimenting with position to find your sweet spot. Don't be afraid to tilt your hips or place the front of your shoulders down onto the bed to get the right angle. Placing your knees further apart and pushing back onto the cock/dildo will assist with deeper penetration. This is a great position for the Sex Goddess who loves the idea of a more submissive role.

If you don't have a partner but still want to explore your A-spot, you can always find the right toy to assist. There are wands and vibrator designed for this purpose. Remember to make sure it has a curved shape designed for this purpose to allow for a more direct stimulation.

You may find that you don't like this form of stimulation during different times of your cycle or you may not even like it at all, and that's ok! It is a matter of experimenting with different positions, times, toys, etc to figure out what works best for you.

SEX GODDESS ACTIVITY

Please turn to Page 60 of your Sex Goddess Workbook now and complete **Challenge 1**.

CHAPTER 23:
ANAL ORGASM

Every sexual encounter is a partnership and agreement to exchange energies and information. The energies and information sent from ourselves to another depend on our level of inner work.

—Shalom Melchizedek, Cosmic Sexuality

THE IDEA OF ANAL play is not so taboo as it once was. It is becoming more and more accepted across different societies. And even though the tides of popularity for anal has increased over the recent years, anal sex has been happening for much longer than many think. We're talking thousands of years. Upbringing, religious beliefs, and even societal misconceptions can play a role in how you view anal play. There is a huge fallacy in the idea that any type of anal play is painful, but this is not necessarily the case. A lot of factors can go into making it painful or pleasurable.

Things such as:

- If the receiving partner is relaxed
- Lubrication
- Size of penetrating object
- Level of arousal
- Pressure
- Single or blended stimulation
- Nerve distribution

Due to the vast amount of nerve endings in the area, that so happen to co-mingle with all those pelvic nerves, anal play has the ability to bring a significant amount of pleasure. As with many of the other orgasms, an anal orgasm is often described and deep full-bodied tingling that builds in intensity, which is often felt in the pussy, including the G-spot providing an elaborate orgasm.

Remember how I said that the nerve bundles from the clit wrap around the vaginal wall, giving it kind of a hug? Well this includes wrapping around to the back wall of the vagina, which is directly in contact with the wall of the rectum. This means in theory anal play can stimulate the same orgasmic nerve bundle, just from a different angle. Many women can cum with just anal stimulation, while many others require a secondary stimulation, which can result in a mind-blowing blended orgasm through clit, vaginal and anal. Imagine all those

THE SEX GODDESS DIARIES

highly sensitive nerves being stimulated from all directions. Talk about intense!

So, what exactly is entailed in anal play, and how do you have an orgasm from it?

Anal play can include anal massage or fingering, analingus (anal-oral stimulation) also known as rimming, or penetration, either with toys or with a penis. There is a small layer between the anus and the vagina, allowing for stimulation of all the nerves in the area during anal play. An orgasm from anal stimulation often feels like deep waves of pleasure radiating throughout your body and can intensify or elicit and a mind-blowing blended orgasm, unleashing repressed sexual energy from our root chakra. If you are ready to explore this exquisite type of orgasm, read on.

How to Prepare

Mentally — Unless you are experienced in this form of sexual pleasure, it is going to be important to take steps and be better prepared for a good experience. One of the first things to do is have a conversation with your partner. Spontaneous sex is awesome, but let me just say I don't recommend it with the booty unless you have talked about it first. Listen to each other concerns, if there are any, without being dismissive.

Once the idea is agreed upon, make sure you discuss how you would like for it to happen. If you only want massage or rimming, say so. If your goal is to work up to full penetration, say that as well. Communication before and during any type of anal play is essential. If you can't talk about it before hand, there is going to be some issues during. Discuss any use of sex toys. Consider buying one together.

Physically — Once the conversation is done and the date is set, you can start to physically prepare. Wash everything up nicely, you can take a hot bath to help relax beforehand. Try doing some gentle anus self-massage as you wash up. The giver should trim nails to reduce risk of any discomfort. Basically, do anything you can to make the experience more comfortable.

Charge any vibrators that you want to use. Make sure there is plenty of anal lube handy.

You can never have too much LUBE!

Warm Up — Remember in our lesson on the Anatomy of an Orgasm I talked about how the central nervous system become fully engaged and the brain starts to release a flow of dopamine? This dopamine leads to a more relaxed state, which in turn is going to help reduce any discomfort. Definitely incorporate more foreplay to heighten arousal! One thing to remember is that anal play, as with most sex, is rarely a solo event. Becoming relaxed and aroused are key to enjoying anal stimulation. The giver should never directly go for it and expect a good response. Anal play is great when incorporated into erotic massages. Once wet and worked up, it is time to start the booty play. The absolute number one thing to remember?

LUBE! LUBE! And MORE LUBE!

Be messy, sling it all over your ass! Just make sure to use plenty of it. Outside of licking or rimming, lube will need to be incorporated into every other aspect when it comes to the booty. Not having enough lube is unquestionably the primary culprit of discomfort during anal play. Now that you've got your body warmed up and humming with foreplay and you're lubed up, let's move into technique.

Fingers

Use of the fingers to stimulate an anus is the most common approach for beginners. It can be as simple as the doorbell method. To do this, use your finger tip to gently press against the anus as if you were ringing a doorbell. You can do it repeatedly, at different speeds, and adjust pressure to whatever feels the best. This can be done by yourself or with a partner. Most everyone who is accepting on the thought of exploring the anus finds this basic technique very enjoyable.

Another finger technique is Circling. This can be done internally or externally. Just move you finger in a small circular motion using the pad of the finger. Start slow and increase speed and pressure as well until you find the sweet spot.

The Come-Hither technique is popular among both men and women. To perform this one, insert a finger into the anus, palm facing the front of the body, and begin to move your finger in a come-hither motion as if beckoning someone to you. As with everything anal, start slow and build intensity and the arousal increases.

The Hummingbird techniques can be done during any of the other strokes usually near climax. Pick whichever of the above methods are most pleasurable and do it ever so slightly, at a very rapid pace, as if your finger were vibrating. If you have ever watched how a hummingbird just seems to be fluttering so quickly yet barely moving, then you get the concept here.

Full Penetration
If you think you're ready for more grab a penis or sex toy and of course, more lube! As with anything anal, the key to an enlightening experience is relaxation, good communication and the need to go slow to help reduce any discomfort.

With any of the finger techniques discussed above, the giving partner, as a rule, was more in control of the action. This should be the opposite with anal penetration. For beginners I suggest getting in a position that is most comfortable to you and gently work your way onto the toy or cock, while continuing to stimulate your clit or anything else that feels good. Remember to breathe deeply during this process as this will help relax the muscles in the anus. The giver should never push or force any object into the anus. Encourage the receiving partner to breathe deeply

Anal play can be done in most sex positions. The one that most everyone thinks of is doggy style as this amply allows access to the ass while providing a full view to the giving partner. But this may not work best for everyone, or if you are trying to masturbate. Different positions allow for how much depth and speed of penetration there is, while usually giving one person more control. Let's go over some of the positions.

Doggy Style — The obvious first thought is doggy style. Like I said it provides access to the ass that makes it easy. Either partner with this one can have the control. This position makes it fairly easy to slowly work your way back onto the cock/toy, as long as your partner is patient. There is also great access to the clit that can help with skyrocketing arousal with dual stimulation. Whether you are on all fours or have your chest down with ass in the air will also help determine angle and depth.

Cowgirl — This one leaves the receiver in more control. Have your partner lay back then straddle them with a leg on either side. With a slow and controlled motion ease down onto the cock or dildo. You can decide the depth and speed with this position through the position of your upper body and hips. Lean forward over your partner, face to face for less penetration and more intimacy, or sit up for a full depth experience. Anal can also be done in a reverse cowgirl position as well but this is for those with more experince.

Lotus — Also known as Yab Yum in Tantra, provides a deep an intimate experience, it doesn't matter if it is in the anus or the pussy, or even just sitting in the position with each other breathing. The giving partner should be sitting in a comfortable supported position, such as on a bed or couch, while the receiver climbs into the partners lap, and slowly slides down onto their cock to initiate penetration. Take your time, adjust as necessary, and don't forget to breathe. The receiving partner should be given control in this position as well, adjusting the depth and pressure.

Side Lying — Laying on your side next to each other, spooning if you will. The receiving partner laying in front of the giving partner. The receiver will bring their free leg up towards their chest, allowing exposure of the anus. The giving partner can then start to stimulate the anus while the receiving can reach down and play with their clit or pussy, allowing for increased stimulation and pleasure.

The Pike Position — Also called a Full Throttle. This one is for the more advanced players. To attain this position, think about a pike dive from swimming. The person is bent in half at the waist with their legs up by their heads in a perfect folded position. Your ass is going to be completely exposed and in control of your partner. It requires a great deal of trust. It gives a deeper fuller penetration, which as the receiver, you don't necessarily have control of the speed or depth. I do not recommend starting with this if you are a beginner. If you are pro at anal, you may have already tried this position and are reading this chapter for fun.

These are just a few of the positions that can be done with anal play. Almost any position can be adjusted for the purpose, it's just going to be finding your preference. One thing to remember is that once you have penetrated the back, with either a cock, toy, or finger you should never return to the vagina unless everything has been cleaned up to prevent any issues. We want it to be fun, but not at the expense of an infection.

I know I have probably said it a million times, but the key things to remember for an enjoyable experience include:

- Communicate with your partner
- Relax
- Breathwork is so important
- Heighten arousal before any anal stimulation
- Go slow
- Adjust pressure and speed as needed
- YOU CAN NEVER HAVE TO MUCH LUBE!

The bottom line is that an anal orgasm can be a ton of fun, and even if you don't have a direct anal orgasm, chances are you will still get to have an orgasm of some kind. You also need to remember that an anal orgasm may not happen the first time. The level of relaxation and comfort play a big role in this. If you are not relaxed, aroused enough, or it is hurting, it is not gonna happen. There is a ton of ways to explore the booty, but playing and figuring out what feels best is half the fun. If anal play is not your thing, that is completely ok! Just keep exploring your body in other ways. But if anal play is intriguing to you, take time to explore this option more. Try using different techniques, pressures, sensations and body parts and put your skills to the test in the quest for the anal orgasm.

SEX GODDESS ACTIVITY

Please turn to Page 61 of your Sex Goddess Workbook now and complete **Challenges 1-2**.

CHAPTER 24:
NIPPLE ORGASM

Breasts are a scandal because they shatter the border between motherhood and sexuality.

—Iris Marion Young

W E LIVE IN A world where anytime sex is discussed people automatically think of genitals. And with good reason. But so often we forget about one of the biggest erogenous zones available to women: their nipples. Due to the large amount of nerve endings found in the nipples, there is an opportunity for an often-untapped source of felicity and climax. The Nipple Orgasm.

So, what exactly is entailed in a nipple orgasm? According to Janet Brito, PhD, a sexologist and clinical psychologist in Honolulu, a nipple orgasms as "a pleasurable release of sexual arousal, centered on nipple stimulation and not caused by stimulating the clitoris or penis directly." Nipple and breast play are often incorporated into sex and foreplay but rarely does it get

102026272829303132

36373940414244454647484950515253545556575859606162636465666768697071727374757677787980818283848586878889909192939495969798991001011021031041051061071081091101111121131141151161171181191201211221231241251261271281291301311321331341351361371381391401411421431441451461471481491501511521531541551561571581591601611621631641651661671681691701711721731741751761771781791801811821831841851861871881891901911921931941951961971981992002012022032042052062072082092102112122132142152162172182192202212222232242252262272282292302312322332342352362372382392402412422432442452462472482492502512522532542552562572582592602612622632642652662672682692702712722732742752762772782792802812822832842852862872882892902912922932942952962972982993003013023033043053063073083093103113123133143153163173183193203213223233243253263273283293303313323333343353363373383393403413423433443453463473483493503513523533543553563573583593603613623633643653663673683693703713723733743753763773783793803813823833843853863873883893903913923933943953963973983994004014024034044054064074084094104114124134144154164174184194204214224234244254264274284294304314324334344354364374384394404414424434444454464474484494504514524534544554564574584594604614624634644654664674684694704714724734744754764774784794804814824834844854864874884894904914924934944954964974984995005015025035045055065075085095105115125135145155165175185195205215225235245255265275285295305315325335345355365375385395405415425435445455465475485495505515525535545555565575585595605615625635645655665675685695705715725735745755765775785795805815825835845855865875885895905915925935945955965975985996006016026036046056066076086096106116126136146156166176186196206216226236246256266276286296306316326336346356366376386396406416426436446456466476486496506516526536546556566576586596606616626636646656666676686696706716726736746756766776786796806816826836846856866876886896906916926936946956966976986997007017027037047057067077087097107117127137147157167177187197207217227237247257267277287297307317327337347357367377387397407417427437447457467477487497507517527537547557567577587597607617627637647657667677687697707717727737747757767777787797807817827837847857867877887897907917927937947957967977987998008018028038048058068078088098108118128138148158168178188198208218228238248258268278288298308318328338348358368378388398408418428438448458468478488498508518528538548558568578588598608618628638648658668678688698708718728738748758768778788798808818828838848858868878888898908918928938948958968978988999009019029039049059069079089099109119129139149159169179189199209219229239249259269279289299309319329339349359369379389399409419429439449459469479489499509519529539549559569579589599609619629639649659669679689699709719729739749759769779789799809819829839849859869879889899909919929939949959969979989991000100110021003100410051006100710081009101010111012101310141015101610171018101910201021102210231024102510261027102810291030103110321033103410351036103710381039104010411042104310441045104610471048104910501051105210531054105510561057105810591060106110621063106410651066106710681069107010711072107310741075107610771078107910801081108210831084108510861087108810891090109110921093109410951096109710981099110011011102110311041105110611071108110911101111111211131114111511161117111811191120112111221123112411251126112711281129113011311132113311341135113611371138113911401141114211431144114511461147114811491150115111521153115411551156115711581159116011611162116311641165116611671168116911701171117211731174117511761177117811791180118111821183118411851186118711881189119011911192119311941195119611971198119912001201120212031204120512061207120812091210121112121213121412151216121712181219122012211222122312241225122612271228122912301231123212331234123512361237123812391240124112421243124412451246124712481249125012511252125312541255125612571258125912601261126212631264126512661267126812691270127112721273127412751276127712781279128012811282128312841285128612871288128912901291129212931294129512961297129812991300130113021303130413051306130713081309131013111312131313141315131613171318131913201321132213231324132513261327132813291330133113321333133413351336133713381339134013411342134313441345134613471348134913501351135213531354135513561357135813591360136113621363136413651366136713681369137013711372137313741375137613771378137913801381138213831384138513861387138813891390139113921393139413951396139713981399140014011402140314041405140614071408140914101411141214131414141514161417141814191420142114221423142414251426142714281429143014311432143314341435143614371438143914401441144214431444144514461447144814491450145114521453145414551456145714581459146014611462146314641465146614671468146914701471147214731474147514761477147814791480148114821483148414851486148714881489149014911492149314941495149614971498149915001501150215031504150515061507150815091510151115121513151415151516151715181519152015211522152315241525152615271528152915301531153215331534153515361537153815391540154115421543154415451546154715481549155015511552155315541555155615571558155915601561156215631564156515661567156815691570157115721573157415751576157715781579158015811582158315841585158615871588158915901591159215931594159515961597159815991600

to be the headliner when it comes to sexual pleasure. Yet nipple orgasms can send sensual waves of pleasure throughout your entire body that feels similar to a clitoris orgasm, but not always as intense. One can often experience a nipple orgasm during erotic massage, because there is a deliberate experience and stimulation provided to the breasts/nipples. Some people have probably had a nipple orgasm, but because the nipple is rarely is coupled with the term orgasm, they may have just not understood what they just experienced.

Of course, it goes without saying that not everyone will want to or be able to experience a nipple orgasm. Everyone has their own level of sensitivity in their nipples and as we all know, it varies at different times of the month. If you have lost sensitivity due to a breast surgery, an injury, breast cancer, or anything that has caused damage to the area, it makes having a nipple orgasm more difficult. If you haven't had any of these, then it is definitely possible, and may just take some work and patience as you explore this realm. Medical studies have shown through functional MRI imaging that nipple stimulation activates the same nerve cortex in your brain that your genitals do. It sends signals up the same pathway to your brain telling it "OOOO! I'm receiving pleasure!" but your brain is not differentiating between clit or nips. It's like all the different orgasm hi-ways merge into one major interstate with the brain

236

being the destination. Intrigued? If so, read on and learn the way of your newest orgasm.

How to Have a Nipple Orgasm

So, you're ready to have your first nipple orgasm? Yay! Let's break it down step by step so you, or your partner, can make those nipples sing!

Set the Scene — If you are looking to have an actual nipple-gasm and not just some boob foreplay, make sure you set the scene, both the physical aspect and your mindset for this purpose. Get everything you may need and have it within reach. This may be massage oils, vibrators, nipple clamps, ice cubes. There is no right or wrong. It is whatever makes you feel like a Sex Goddess. Release any judgment or expectations from your mind. Be ready to openly accept whatever the pleasure may feel like.

Breathwork — Start by calming your mind with the Breath of Bliss and work your way through to circular breath to get the sexual energy flowing. Remember to maintain breathwork through the experience. This will help keep you grounded in the moment.

Warm Up Sexual Energy — I recommend not going directly for the nipple when starting. Like most things sexual, women need some time to warm up to get everything flowing. You may want to get some warmed oil, and drip it on across your breasts and belly. We tend to hold a lot of tension in our tummies and groin areas. Doing a gentle massage in these areas help to release tension and starts to sends pleasure signals to the brain, priming it. You can alternate between your neck, tummy and chest bone with gentle caresses.

Breast Play — Once you feel your body start to respond, use featherlight touches to trace circles around the outer edges of your breasts. Experiment with a variety of touches. Trace your breast with one finger or you can gently massage a larger portion of the breast excluding the nipple at this point. Start to trace the edges of your areola to bring the sensations more central towards the nipple. You can continue going back and forth between massaging the breast and tracing the edges of the areola, building the excitement and anticipation while priming your nipple response. Keep your hands flowing between your body and your breast with featherlight touch, massage, kneading, whatever touch feels good, paying attention to how it feels, drinking in every sensation.

Nipple Play — By the time you this step your nipples should be begging for attention. They may be standing erect with arousal. With one fingertip rub the tip of your nipples in a circular motion, then move back to circular tracings around the areola before moving back to the nipple. Take your nipple between two fingers and roll it back and forth a few times before pinching or tweaking it. This activity will cause your brain to release oxytocin, a hormone that causes us to relax, and is known as the love or cuddle hormone. Work with varying pressures, pinches and tweaks.

Now is the time to start incorporating other sensations into the nipple play. You can use feathers to stroke the nipples gently, moving between them and down to your tummy or neck before circling back. Remember to continue your breathwork during this. You can use ice, or nipple clamps, vibrators or even your partners mouth to stimulate different sensations, alternating between them. Give your partner feedback, ask them to do whatever feels good to you. You can also be touching your body as they shower your nipples with pleasure, allowing them to stimulate both at the same time if you so desire it. They can even nibble on them a bit for pleasure. As you become more aroused, your nipples can handle more intense sensations. The stronger the touch, the more oxytocin is released. You can have your partner deeply roll your nipples between their fingers while flicking the tip with their tongue. Touch your body as they do this.

Build and Release — You can use the same Edging technique here that was taught in the masturbation chapter, building pleasure and intensity. A nipple orgasm is different from a clitoral orgasm as is sends multiple rolling waves of pleasure through the body rather than a focused orgasm. The edging and continued exploration of our body moves our orgasmic energy throughout our body in a wave like pattern. I want you to flow with it. Arch your back pushing your breast forwards whenever you feel the desire. As your nipples continue to be dowsed in pleasure, rock your hips and squeeze your pelvic floor muscles, like doing a Kegel, and release, allowing the energy to flow back towards your breasts. Enjoy the tumultuous waves. It is now up to you how to release. This can be done by continuing with the nipples only, or you can start to stroke your clit. You can even take your lover inside of you. Whatever it is, the experience of ecstasy is at your fingertips. Surrender to it.

Things to Know About Nipple Orgasms

Remember to stay present in the moment. If you feel you mind drifting, focus on your breath and the sensations. Be mindful of how sensitive your nipples are at different times of the month and adjust your nipple massage. Experiment with different sensations. I mentioned using ice, vibrators, nipple clamps, etc. and incorporating them. Find what feels best to you. Remember, nipple orgasms can feel much different than a clit orgasm, but you can incorporate them together. If nipple orgasms are not your thing, that's ok! This is about your journey. Do what feels best to you.

SEX GODDESS ACTIVITY

Please turn to Page 63 of your Sex Goddess Workbook now and complete **Challenge 1**.

CHAPTER 25:
SQUIRTING

The future is female ejaculation.

—Unknown

SQUIRTING — ONE OF THE most controversial topics among women when it comes to their bodies. Over the past several years it has been one of the hottest debates out there. For many women, they feel as if squirting is a mystical (and mythical) phenomenon just portrayed in porn, often wondering if it is even an actual thing. Others think it is just women peeing on themselves. I can tell you from experience, it is neither.

Let me just say up front that while squirting is not an orgasm in itself it just felt like the orgasm section of the book was the best place to put it. Know that while still pleasurable for most women, squirting provides a different, often intense, sensation from orgasm, and can accompany orgasms or happen independently.

So, what is squirting — or female ejaculation exactly? Well according to medical research, female ejaculation occurs when a woman expels a fluid from her Skene's glands that, when looked at under a microscope, is not urine, but actually a fluid that is very similar the same fluid produced by the prostate gland in men. Analysis has shown that the expelled fluid contains prostatic acid phosphatase (PSA) which is an enzyme present in male semen that helps sperm motility, and that the female ejaculate also contains fructose, just as in male semen. It can be a milky white, containing high amounts of PSA and fructose, or clear watery and odorless, having lower amounts of PSA and fructose. Fructose as we know is a form of sugar, and according to one study in 2014, the fluid released during female ejaculation has a sweet taste to it. So, the fact that it was dubbed "nectar of the gods" in ancient India, makes for a very fitting representation. This may be why some people love the taste when going down on a woman.

Looking back at our anatomy section, you will remember that the Skene's glands are located in the front, inside wall of the vagina near the G-spot. Researchers believe that stimulation of the glans is this area causes the female make and excrete ejaculate fluid, which then move into the urethra that is then expelled, thus giving the sensation of urination.

How Common Is it?

According to The International Society of Sexual Medicine upwards of 50% of women have experiences squirting, while OMGyes.com indicates that 41% of women who have participated in their research have experienced squirting, many who spent years thinking it was not possible before it actually happened. What is known for sure about female ejaculation, is that the feelings, triggers, and amount of fluid expelled, varies considerably from between women.

It is my personal opinion that more women are capable of squirting. They either just don't know they can, like those who participated with OMGyes, they have a fear of doing it, don't understand how to make it happen, or are just plain putting too much pressure on themselves to perform.

So, as a Sex Goddess, the question remains:

To Squirt?

OR

Not to Squirt?

And the answer, my lovely Goddess, is that it's completely up to you. My purpose is to give you the knowledge on how to pursue and achieve the act of squirting, if you so desire.

Becoming Comfortable

Now, one of the most pressing things we need to talk about to be able to squirt is the concept that women think or feel like they are peeing themselves. As we have already discussed that this is not the case, you have to move beyond the embarrassment to embrace the idea of squirting. Anything that you are not comfortable with sexually, you will most likely not be able to achieve. If you have to much anxiety about any part of it, whether it be about your capabilities, what your partner thinks, or even the possibility of the mess, that anxiety will make it just that much more difficult.

So, the very first step to squirting is to become comfortable with the idea. Learn more about it! Identify any fears or concerns you have. And then prepare. I implore you, that if squirting is something that you want to do, or if you can already but want to understand it better, go to OMGyes.com, where it is covered in Season 2. Watching those videos by those amazing women is incredibly helpful.

How to Squirt

It is suggested that there is a commonality in the approach to be able to achieve squirting. It includes a consistent, tension building stimulation, followed a trigger or release. OMGyes describes it as Ramp Rub Release.

Let's break it down:

RAMP: Find the area of stimulation, usually towards the front vaginal wall where the G-spot is most commonly located. Some women prefer to do this with a direct clit stimulation. Use different forms of stimulation to see what works best for you to build tension. We are looking for the area to stimulate that will sensation of needing to pee. This can give you a clue that you are on the right track. This area that you have identified is probably going to need some prolonged or intense stimulation. To do this start with a gentle massage to warm the area up and then gradually ramp up the intensity, pressure, and speed.

RUB: This is where you become consistent in your motions, maintaining the intensity, pressure, and speed, which is often achieved with a repetitive pumping or fucking sensation. It may require harder or faster stimulation than you might expect, and for longer than normal, but keep it consistent. Don't slow down, don't stop. Don't change position. Any disruption will lead a decrease in the stimulation of the glands and may need to start over. Every time I have squirted it has been during that amazing hard pounding sex that just keeps going and going and I just can't get enough! The more he kept going, the more I was able to squirt.

RELEASE: The release happens after you have built up so much tension that you feel like you may burst and you really feel like you might pee yourself. Here are some techniques that have been shared by women that can be used to explore this concept. They can be done as a single act or combined together to stimulate a release, or squirting.

- Super Consistency — This means there is no change in what you were doing during the RUB portion. It entails continuing a complete, consistent, and intense motion, which works well for me. Approximately 15% of women can achieve squirting with consistency.

- Unclenching Muscles — This technique provides 21% of women the ability to squirt after a good RUB. To do it, just consciously relax the muscles, which have bene clenched for some time during the RUB. Imaging a water balloon that you have been filling with water and at just the right moment when you think it won't hold any more, you let go of it, and the water flows out. Woosh!!

- Bear Down — A total of 13% of women are able to squirt when they bear down on their pelvic floor muscles; you know the ones we all do Kegels with? Imaging the same water balloon but this time it is just barely tied, then when you apply pressure to that balloon, it pops open and water squirts out everywhere!

- Sudden Bursts of Speed — A whopping 17% of women report squirting after, after what seems like their limit during rubbing, there is a sudden burst of increased speed and pressure. This happens only after the initial pressure is built. Now we have put an excessive amount of pressure on the water balloon and it goes POP! (note: you will not hurt or pop anything during this, it's just a metaphor for visualization purposes.)
- Withdrawal — Up to 10% of women report that they squirt when something, such as a toy or a dick, is pulled out of their vagina, causing a release similar to unclenching the muscles. The plug has been taken out and the fluid is released!

I personally love a good combination of these techniques, but the super consistency, the sudden bursts of speed and the withdrawal all can cause me to squirt. Every time I have squirted during sex it has been during that amazing hard pounding sex that just keeps going and going and I just can't get enough, allowing me to squirt multiple times!

Things To Know About Squirting

The amount of fluid released can vary from between each experience and is different for each woman. According to one study completed in 2013, the amount of fluid released during female ejaculation can range from a few drops up to more than half a cup! It can dribble, flow out in a quick gush or even shoot across the room! **All of which are normal**.

The feeling like you are peeing yourself is going to seem very real. Just remember everything you have learned and know that squirting is a scientifically proven different experience from urination. To help ease the worry you may consider going to the bathroom right before sex to ensure that your bladder is empty prior. In my experience, I am much more aware of this sensation when I squirt with masturbation rather than with sex. And it definitely feels similar to pressure from needing to pee, although I know it is different. You need to be able to trust your body. Focus on what is feeling amazing.

Don't be surprised if it takes multiple tries before you are able to squirt. And it *definitely* doesn't happen every single time. It doesn't mean that you are doing anything wrong. It may just take practice and persistence to learn how your body responds.

There will most likely be a mess. You have to completely and totally embrace the "nectar" spilling over. To fully experience female ejaculation, you must be willing to let go, psychologically, emotionally, and physically, in a way that may be a little scary a first, but then allows you to be a liberated Sex Goddess reveling in ecstasy and sweet delicious fluids, or Goddess Honey if you will.

Toys

Don't feel bad if you want to try doing with a toy first over a partner. Many women feel that they have a bit more control by doing so, while others say this is the only way they can squirt. Trying to achieve squirting on your own can be challenging unless you have the right toy. Often there is not enough of an angle, and the area to stimulate is deeper, making it difficult for you to hold a toy that is not designed for this in the right spot. Plus, you have to have enough consistency of stimulation to squirt, so holding a toy at an awkward angle, a squirt it does not make. The use of a vibrator vs manual wands is totally going to be a preference. The wands may require more handwork, but both can get the job done.

While there are several options out there in the toy world designed to hit the G-spot area, one that has been very effective is the Pure Wand from NJoy. It is an 8 in curved stainless-steel G-spot stimulator that is known for getting the job done. Find one that has the right curve for you!

Squirting Is Not For Everyone
As with anything sexual, this may just not be your thing. And that's ok! You may either just not be able to do it, or you may be part of the 14% of women out there who say that while the have squirted before, they did not find enjoyment out of it. The Sex Goddess knows her realm and accepts it as it makes her whole.

SEX GODDESS ACTIVITY

Please turn to Page 64 of your Sex Goddess Workbook now and complete **Challenges 1-4**.

CHAPTER 26:
PROSTATE ORGASM

*The most unfair thing about sex is that men are almost always
guaranteed an orgasm.*

—Mokokoma Mokhonoana

THE G-SPOT FOR MEN. The internal Million
Dollar Point. The orgasm that so many
straight men fear, yet desperately need to
experience. I am talking about a prostate orgasm.
Remember that little walnut shaped part of the male
anatomy? It is time to become intimately familiar with
it.

First off, let me start by saying before you attempt
any form of prostate massage, I recommend discussing
and setting boundaries, wishes and any concerns. Decide
together to do only what feels comfortable and respect
each other.

Okay. Are you ready?

You already know and are familiar with the male
ejaculatory orgasm. But here we are going to talk about

how to give a prostate orgasm. If your guy is unwilling to explore his prostate, then he is seriously losing out on a whole new level of mind-blowing blissful full–bodied orgasms that goes way beyond his dick. The biggest block to having mind-blowing prostate orgasms is mental resistance. The mental preparation is super important in this journey for a man. As a Sex Goddess, you play a big part in the mental prep.

When stimulated correctly, men have the potential to have a prostate orgasm, and they can have this orgasm without ever ejaculating. This means that a man can become multi-orgasmic as well. The experience usually does not result in an orgasm on the first try, though it is a possibility. It may take some time, relaxation and different techniques to get there. And communication. A lot of communication. You can't just go and stick a finger up his butt and expect him to have a magical mid-blowing experience. It has to go through a process called milking the prostate. But once a man learns to let go and how to have one, It often becomes easier to achieve the next one.

Beyond the orgasm, there can be some health benefits as well. Enough so that proctologists often recommend prostate milking to their patients. Regularly stimulating the area can help to strengthen his pelvic floor muscles. Stimulating the prostate can also flush out the gland and has even be shown help reduce the risk for prostate cancer.

In addition to these physical health benefits, prostate orgasms allow a new type of pleasure experience and may even induce a state of ecstasy in a man and can add a whole new dimension to your sexual experiences.

So, what, exactly, does a prostate orgasm feel like? Well many men report that the prostate orgasm goes beyond his dick, kind of like a full out of body orgasmic experience. And while regular orgasms are intense but brief, the prostate orgasm feels similar to the beginning of a normal orgasm only more intense and it can last a very long time. It uses a term called "riding the wave" because the sensation continues to ripple throughout the body. And because men can experience a prostate orgasm without ejaculation the experience itself can continue as long as he can. For an ultimate experience he can have both a prostate orgasm and a normal ejaculatory orgasm simultaneously! I personally don't know why any man would want to say no to that experience.

So how exactly do you get him there? Well first you gotta know where to find the prostate. So, if we go back to our anatomy lessons, you will remember that the only way to directly stimulate the prostate in through the rectum, which is why so many men resist the idea. Indirectly it can be stimulated through that "Million-

Dollar point" in the perineum, which hopefully you have been stroking during his penis massages. Start off with whatever he is comfortable with.

How to Find a Prostate

The prostate is about an inch wide and has a firm feel with some slight give. The prostate should be fairly easy to find as it feels distinct from the rectum. As a man becomes aroused, his prostate with swell and become firmer and more prominent making it that much easier to find.

I would suggest trying to find the prostate externally first. To do this, have him lay on his back and feel in his perineum between his scrotum and his anus, gently pressing down as you feel. You should be able to feel a firm bulge. This is the prostate, aka "the Million-Dollar point". You can begin to stroke this area using your fingers or a toy, whatever is most pleasurable to your partner. If he is open to the idea of a prostate orgasm you may try and gently stroke the Million-Dollar point as a single act, having him revel in the pleasure and give you directions on how much pressure to apply and where. If he is still not 100% on board, you may just add the external stroking of his prostate while having some penis play as well, taking some of the taboo edge off while still experiencing pleasure. I suggest massaging the Million-Dollar point on a few separate occasions prior to milking the prostate directly. This act in itself, with practice, can become very pleasurable and can induce a prostate orgasm.

Once your fella has become comfortable with the idea, it's time to move on to directly stimulating the prostate. Now here's a super important part. You are going to need a high-quality lube. My preference is Uber Lube, but any good quality lube will do. Don't get a cheap one that dries out quickly. You may want to elect to get a lubricant specifically formulated for anal play. These products will have a thicker consistency that lasts longer, so you won't need to reapply as often. Oil or silicone-based lubricants may last longer than water-based, but they're harder to clean up. Water-based lubricants are compatible with all sex toys, but need to be reapplied more often than oil or silicone-based types.

Positions

Before we go into a full prostate massage, let's go over some positions. There are a few different options here, and as with every other aspect of the prostate massage, you must find what is most comfortable for your partner.

Here are some positions to try:

- Laying Back: As we discussed in the Million Dollar point external massage, a popular position for a full prostate massage is to lay back in a comfortable position. This one usually makes men feel the most in control while allowing full access to his penis as well. Sometimes you may have an easier time finding their prostate when they lift their legs closer to their chest.

- Face Down: Needless to say, lying face down leaves men feeling more vulnerable but his anus in a much more approachable position allowing for an easier access to reach the prostate.

- The Side Lay: If you are looking for a middle ground approach you may want to have him lay on his side and brings his knees towards his chest. This can make the prostate easier to reach for you.

Prostate Massage

Make sure your mate is aroused prior to starting. You'll need to apply some lube to his anus, making sure it is warm prior to applying. You can warm it simply by rubbing it around in hour fingers for a minute beforehand. Then make sure you have plenty of lube on your finger as well.

Don't immediately start inserting your finger. I would rub the perineum area with your thumb, while gently pressing against his anus. Pulse you finger against his anus, asking for feedback on the pressure and how it feels. You want him to relax as much as possible before inserting your finger. If he is not relaxed, the anus is going to be tense, and any attempt at insertion is going to be painful. Remember you want this to be a pleasurable experience for him. Continue to touch him with your other hand, rub his thighs, penis, whatever makes him feel good.

There are a few ways to go about inserting your finger. I recommend that a man who is first starting out with this sexual realm, to make sure he is being stimulated in secondary way. This may mean giving him a hand job or sucking on his dick at the same time of insertion. A man who has not experienced having his prostate milked before, the act by itself is probably going to be too much. The key in any of this is going to be communication. Keep looking for his cues, ask him what he wants and what feels good.

Ask your partner to do some slow in and out deep breathes. Hopefully you have taught him the Breath of Bliss which can be very useful here. As you are pulsing his anus, do it in rhythm with his exhalation, each time pressing more each time. Communicate when you are going to insert your finger and ask him to take a bid deep breath and slowly exhale as you insert your finger.

To locate the prostate internally, you will have to insert most of your finger into his rectum. Turn your hand with the palm facing towards his belly side. Start gently feeling around for a firm walnut sized bulge. When you press against it, he may feel like he needs to urinate, this is a normal response. This should always be as gentle as possible in the beginning. More pressure and intensity can be added with experience. Allow him time to become familiar with different sensations.

Once you know where the prostate is located it's time to start the massage. There really isn't a right or wrong way to massage a prostate as long as it feels good to your partner. Some men like a quick thrusting while other like a simple more direct pressure. Experiment to see what feels best. In general, the prostate tends to respond to a repetitive, firm pressure. Start out soft and increase intensity as you go. Fingers are a good place to start with prostate massage, but in the long run they may not be as adequate to getting the job done as a toy when more experience is in play. I recommend starting off with finger then if he is comfortable, moving on to a toy. There are toys available on the market that are made specifically for this purpose, and the use of a toy may increase a man's ability to experience a full prostate orgasm. For the fingers though, there are a few tried and true techniques that have been found to be effective.

Some techniques you can start with include:

- Circular Movements: Move your fingers in a circular motion around the prostate switching between small or big circles.
- Stroking: The second technique you can try is stroking. To do this imagine that you're using your finger in a "come here" motion and continually stroke the prostate.
- Pressing: This one is straight forward. You can stimulate the prostate gland by pressing on it. Start gentle and apply more pressure to a level that is still pleasurable.

Prostate Milking

Once a prostate has been stimulated for a while the prostate may feel firmer and you may notice that the penis starts leaking the milky white fluid that makes up a large portion of the semen. Remember this fluid is made in the prostate. This is where the term "prostate milking" comes from.

For many, milking is a sign that you may be nearing orgasm.

Reaching the Big P.O.

The almighty prostate orgasm. The goal which we have been working for. Her we are going to discuss ways to get your man on that wave.

Hopefully by now you have had some awesome sessions building trust and intense pleasure with prostate massage. One of the things that ends to hold men back is that urge they feel when their prostate is being massaged, like they need to go to the bathroom. Many of them fear they are going to wet themselves due to this sensation. Assure them that this is a good sign leading to the orgasm. As a routine, have him completely empty his bladder prior to any prostate massage to help alleviate some fear. Plus, if you have open communication about it, it will help alleviate any fears. Encourage him to push past this urge to pull back and fall into the release of orgasm.

Another technique to help him reach orgasm is to use the Edging technique we learned in masturbation. This is most often done with a dual stimulation of the penis and the prostate. In some cases, you can bring him near the edge or ejaculation with penile stimulation prior to any prostate massage (this ensures a good arousal starting point), but you can also do it, or even have him masturbate while you perform prostate massage. Whatever it takes to help him reach this mind-altering full-body ecstasy inducing orgasm. If he is stroking himself, and you are stroking his prostate, a little buzz of a vibrator on that Million-Dollar Point may just be the thing that pushes him over the edge!

He's not into it. Now what?

If you have done everything you can to make him comfortable but he still not into, that's ok! Let it go. Not every man can enjoy a prostate massage.

He may just need some more time to digest what's happening to become comfortable, but then again, he may just not be able to relax enough to get there. Either way, respect that, just as you would want to be respected.

Prostate Massagers

As mentioned before, having a prostate massager can add a significant amount of pleasure for those who are open to trying them. These toys are designed specifically to stimulate the prostate and are therefore more comfortable.

And since they're designed specifically for anal use, prostate massagers will have a handle or flared base making them safer to use without fear of losing it up there. Prostate massagers come in all shapes and types, and are designed to fit around or sit on the prostate. Another advantage to using a prostate massager is the added vibrations. This extra stimulation may be exactly what it is needed to reach that cosmic prostate orgasm. As always, before inserting anything into the anus make sure you apply plenty of lube both to the tool and your anus allowing for a silky-smooth entry. Insert it with the curve facing upward towards your stomach just like your finger would be curved in the "come here" position.

To view my choice for an awesome prostate massager, check out this link:

http://lip.go2cloud.org/SHsy

You can also find a selection my website at serenaskinner.com

Prep Note:

For those who need instruction on how to prep for prostate play, read on. This is for the beginners and those who want to take a few extra steps.

So, one of the first and most basic prep step you can take for prostate massage, or any anal play, is to clear out the rectum by having a bowel movement. This will ensure a cleaner experience and make it less likely that you'll encounter any feces in the rectum. You can take a shower, washing the anal area with soap and water.

If there is a big concern ensuring a clean experience you can use an anal douche to flush out your rectum. These can be purchased on Amazon. This tool will basically flush any products out of the rectum using warm water. It may also be helpful to get any large amounts of lube out as well.

Make sure nails are clean and short, with no rough edges. It may make one or both of you more comfortable if you use a glove (the kind you find in the doctor's office) during any finger insertion into the anus.

SEX GODDESS ACTIVITY

Please turn to Page 68 of your Sex Goddess Workbook now and complete **Challenge 1**.

CHAPTER 27:
BECOMING MULTI-ORGASMIC

If not you, then who? If not now, when?"

—Hillel First- Century Jewish Scholar

S O, WHAT DOES IT mean to be a multi-orgasmic Sex Goddess?
Well this is up to you. It can be a multitude of spine shivering orgasms back to back. Or it can be that one that even seems to be an ongoing wave during that hot and crazy sex. But it can also be a slow and intentional approach of building and edging that allows you to experience different kinds of orgasms. All of these approaches allow you to explore a deeper realm of ecstasy within yourself.

If you haven't read the previous chapters, I implore you to go back and read them. Also make sure you have access to OMGYes.com and have watched some of the videos. You are going to find TONS of pointers on how to get the most out of this chapter.

How long it takes to become multi-orgasmic again is going to be up to you. Some women make it there in a few days and others a few months. Where you are in your sexuality journey when you start this aspect plays a big role. We can't expect two women to have the same sexual journey.

Many times, we have barriers, physically or mentally that keep us from being multi-orgasmic, or orgasmic at all for that matter. Most often our barriers may be self-imposed.

For example, if you currently are only able to reach orgasm with a vibrator, that could mean that you have trained yourself mentally to accept this. Or if you have a certain expectation of what an orgasm is supposed to feel like, you may not notice a more subtle one or accept it. If you are judging yourself on the way you sound or look you are definitely limiting yourself to experiencing the full realm of orgasm.

So, the first thing I want you to do is stop and identify what is your current orgasm style by answering the following questions.

- Are you able to orgasm most of the time?
- Do you reach orgasm the same way each time, such as with clit stimulation?
- Can you reach orgasm several times a day?
- Are you able to have different kinds of orgasms?

- Can you identify how different kinds of orgasms feel individually?
- Do you feel rushed to complete an orgasm once you feel it coming on?
- Do you worry about how you sound or look?

Make a commitment right now to step outside of your comfort zone. Put aside your current orgasm style for the next 30 days and find new ways to reach bliss. Put away the vibrator if that has been your go to way to orgasm! Keep it slow and controlled if you tend to rush it. Be open to sounding erotic. Go back over the last several chapters and delve into learning the different techniques.

I want you to believe that this can happen! Orgasms are as simply a stimulation of the nervous system as we learned in chapter 20. A domino effect of signals transmitted throughout your body. We are able to train our bodies on a multitude of levels to attain physical fitness. If you believe that you can train your muscles by working out, you can damn sure bet that you can train your nervous system to attain multiple orgasms. It's time to train like a pro athlete! Put in the work and dedication to make things happen! You can do this in solo play but it is also very fun with a partner. Having a good and patient partner makes the process flow that much easier. But you need to *want* to be multi-orgasmic for it to happen. You have to allow the sexual energy to ebb and flow through you, be willing to go outside your comfort zone if needed, push beyond. Be ready to surrender, let go of expectations, and of course, breathe. (All of this should be sounding familiar by now right!) It is also important to remember that there is more than one way to orgasm as we have learned. Experiencing each one individually can help you identify what each one feels like so that hopefully you know when you are having more than one at the same time.

SEX GODDESS ACTIVITY

Please turn to Page 69 of your Sex Goddess Workbook now and complete **Challenge 1-2**.

CONCLUSION

THE JOURNEY OF THE Sex Goddess is never complete: life challenges us and, in turn, changes who we are on a regular basis. The sexuality we experience at age 20 is very different than that we experience at age 40, 60, 70 and beyond. We, as humans, are fluid in who we are throughout life—meaning our sexuality must be, too! The power and energy that we hold demand that the journey continues. We owe it to the divine in each of us to honor this process; to live in it each day; to be grateful for the process and the journey.

I can only hope that this book is just the beginning for you, and that you continue to explore your divine sexuality on a daily basis; indeed, this book has provided you with the foundations required in order for you to begin your personal exploration into what it means to be a Sex Goddess. Your path is going to be different from the person sitting next to you; we each have different partners and life experiences, and we each make different choices. What feels good to you, someone else may hate, and vice versa. Our bodies are glorious and beautiful;

different yet the same; each of us possessing deeper capabilities than we previously believed.

What you have learned in this process of becoming a Sex Goddess is the ability to love yourself fully, in body and spirit, as well as how to drop the misogynistic notions that have suffocated your sexuality. You have learned that having a tribe is essential in the journey, providing love and support on a deeper level and having bonds that will pull you out of your darkest hour in any aspect of life. You have learned about your greatest gift—sexual energy—, and how, when used properly, it can transcend beauty across your life. You have also learned that attaining ecstasy is achieved in the process through breathwork, released fears, self-love, and the willingness to be vulnerable in the moment. You have also learned more about your body and your partners', and how they work to help you reach your sexual goals. The pursuit of pleasure is founded in knowledge, and in line with this, you have discovered different realms of pleasure, both as a solo player or with a partner. You should now be able to understand the importance of masturbation, and hopefully have done the work to discover your sexuality more deeply through different techniques. You have also come to know how masturbation can keep sexual energy flowing without the need for a partner.

You have discovered new ways to connect with and pleasure your partner through mind connection, an erotic massage, and a pussy/penis massage, allowing for a more intimate and sexually mind-blowing experience. The possibilities are endless in terms of ways to connect.

You have also discovered that there are more ways to orgasm than you likely ever thought possible!

The body is the ultimate playground to an enlightened experience through orgasm and ecstasy, and having so many options to take you there should be exciting! I believe one should always look for the next level of their sexuality.

Communication, consent, and acceptance are the three big components in embracing this journey with a partner; nothing should be done to either you or a partner without these. Overall, however, as an individual, true love and acceptance of yourself as a beautiful and amazing woman is what I hope you have found during this process more than anything.

Reality is that you wield the most divine power known to humankind in your beautiful, enticing, exquisite pussy; it is the most sacred gift, and *you* possess it!

I do hope you take the time to nurture the Sex Goddess in you beyond this book. I have yet to meet a woman who has regretted it! We, as women, have so much to gain (and so much to give!) by embracing our divine sexuality and exploring it on a deeper level. I wish you a lifetime of intimacy, an abundance of sexual energy and health, and a joyful mind full of self-loving thoughts and acceptance.

YOUR WORKBOOK

As a reminder, you can download your copy of the Sex Goddess Workbook right here!

https://app.serenaskinner.com/sexgoddesswb

CPSIA information can be obtained
at www.ICGtesting.com
Printed in the USA
FSHW021151021220
76377FS